P9-BJU-550

The ompetitive ntelligence
Handbook

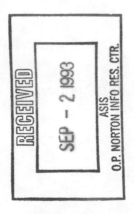
Richard E. Combs
John D. Moorhead

The Scarecrow Press, Inc.
Metuchen, N.J., & London   1992

British Library Cataloguing-in-Publication data available

Library of Congress Cataloging-in-Publication Data

Combs, Richard E.
  The competitive intelligence handbook / by Richard E.
Combs, John D. Moorhead.
    p.   cm.
  Includes bibliographical references and index.
  ISBN 0-8108-2606-2 (alk. paper)
  1. Business intelligence--Handbooks, manuals, etc.
  2. Competition--Handbooks, manuals, etc.
I. Moorhead, John D. 1941– . II. Title.
HD38.7.C657 1992
658.4'7–dc20
                                   92-32740

And so the prince returned from the Valley of Promise and sorrowfully made his way back to the king, his father, for he had failed in his first quest and was sorely afraid he would never be permitted to make another.

"Mercy, Father," he cried, falling on one knee and reluctantly holding forth his sword. "I am not to blame. The evil gatekeeper put me on the wrong road, and I lost my horse. Then the forest people drugged me with wine, and I lost my strength. The very page you gave me was in the service of the dragon. The dragon himself was unrecognizable. And the maiden proved, in sooth, to be no maiden. Surely such hazards are beyond all reason. The contest was not fair."

"It never is," said the king, taking his sword.

A Packet of Fairy Tales[*]
Anonymous

---

[*] Kelly, Robert Glynn, **A Lament for Barney Stone**, New York, NY, Holt, Rinehart and Winston, 1961, p. 205.

Table of contents

In **The Competitive Intelligence Handbook** we have
spelled out our own approach to competitive intelligence
work, and delineated other approaches to the discipline as
we understand them. As independent practitioners we
have a unique point of view which brings with it both the
limitations and blessings of this role.

This independent status has allowed us a freedom we
cherish, and has also shaped our vision of the field of
competitive intelligence and business research, a vision
reflected throughout this book. The freedom has also
allowed us to make mistakes, though in all modesty we
have not made many, and to try some things we might not
have tried otherwise. Many of the successes we've enjoyed
would not have taken place in the confines of a less
forgiving organization, nor would the learning have been
as intense. We've tried, in **The Competitive Intelligence
Handbook**, to pass along much of what we've learned
about the business of competitive intelligence.

Regrettably, what cannot be passed along in these pages is
an attitude toward the work that one of our favorite clients
describes as a "dogged and unswerving pursuit of the
answer." It seems to us that this drive to get at the truth of
things shapes our work as much as anything. For some
years we thought everybody did it this way, but apparently not.

One of the authors, John Moorhead, was for a time an
intelligence officer with the U.S. Navy on board the aircraft
carriers Independence and Franklin Delano Roosevelt, and
later worked as a staff reporter for *The Christian Science
Monitor*. All this work established in his mind the importance and power of information.

Richard Combs has a research/writing background, and worked as a library director in a number of municipal libraries, starting with the Newport, R.I., "People's Library" and ending with the Chicago Public Library Cultural Center. Working with the research needs of any community quickly persuades you of the importance of information to everyone; older and younger students, business people, and academics. As intelligent beings, information is the air we breathe. Without it, our lives are impoverished, our power diminished.

Working as a chief administrator in the public sector during those years also made me realize that information does cost money. Those who believe that public library information is "free"–one of the great wrong ideas of our time, certainly–should spend a moment reflecting on the origins of their community's tax base. (Don't forget to add to the cost of that reference question the cost of the library building, staff salaries and health insurance costs.)

We have had our own business research/competitive analysis firm, CombsMoorhead Associates Inc., in Chicago, since 1983.

One of our first corporate brochures displayed a line drawing of a penguin with the legend, "He knows everything he needs to know to get through the day." Unfortunately *homo sapiens* is not so blessed. Since we aren't "hard–wired" with the necessary information to get us through our professional or personal lives, we need to learn things. As Samuel Johnson observed, "Curiosity is one of the permanent and certain characteristics of a vigorous mind." Fortunately our client base is shaped by these characteristics: they **do not** already know what they need to know to get through the day, and they are profoundly curious about the world around them.

Whether "they" are a marketer in an international corporation, an account executive with an public relations firm, or a trial attorney, they perceive the pool of world knowledge as something to gain from, and they turn to us for our understanding of the paths of access to this pool. Our expertise in business information and competitive intelligence simply lies in our understanding of the ways to get at information. We have tried, in this book, to spell out these pathways as we understand them.

We hope the book will be useful to a wide range of users, from the novice and the more experienced practitioner to the student seeking a broader understanding of the craft. It may even prove useful to that hardy soul about to set up shop as a business researcher/broker.

The book itself has two primary thrusts:

- information on the discipline of competitive intelligence itself—how the work can be done, how it ought to be done, and how it usually is done.

- sources of primary and secondary information upon which competitive intelligence professionals rely.

The first focus, on books about competitive intelligence, is not often done in the existing literature about CI. We felt that a significant number of books—and books from different perspectives—have been written about CI at this point in time, and that a comparative discussion of these books might be useful to the reader as a further orientation to the field.

The second focus of the book, on sources of competitive intelligence information, has been written about extensively. Several guides to such information resources are already available, but we have included those titles we have found to be most useful in our own work.

Because some still wrongly think of competitive intelligence as "cloak and dagger", we want to stress that the information gathering methods discussed in this book are ethical and legal. Nothing else is necessary to succeed. On this point, at least, there is broad agreement in the field.

Portions of this book appeared previously in *Database* magazine, the **Encyclopedia for Library and Information Science** (Volume 49), and in the newsletter *Competitor Intelligence*; they are used by permission.

The ideas presented here took shape over years of work with many skilled and knowledgeable people it has been our pleasure to know. But three deserve our thanks here. Our gratitude goes to Patrice Moran, whose singular talents in design and typography have given this book its distinctive appearance. Her energy, industry and humor have been invaluable in making this book a reality. Margaret Jasinski provided timely editorial guidance. Franklin Orwin–our astute advisor–provided his usual wisdom, tact and willingness to pitch in.

One brief typographical note. We have used UPPER CASE lettering for database acronyms and database gateway acronyms (as in DIALOG), and to distinguish between book titles (**Standard & Poor's** vs. STANDARD & POOR'S) and database names, a **bold** typeface to denote book titles, and an *italic bold* for periodical titles. In those cases where a newspaper is also the name of a database, we have used an *italic bold*.

An overview of competitive intelligence

One of the first lessons the novice must learn is that stupidity is no mere passive misfortune but a sin—active, aggressive, sensual in its enjoyment, and jealous of its self-preservation, being rooted, like all sins, in a corruption not primarily of the intellect but of the will.

A Manual of Spiritual Exercises
Anon., c. 1490 (Translated by E.C. Hart)[1]

Competitive intelligence has undergone a groundswell of interest in recent years, an interest in part fueled by the increasing availability of information itself—the much touted information explosion—and an increase reflected in the proliferation of commercial databases world-wide. What else is driving this growth?

Fig. 1.1

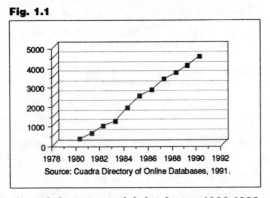

Source: Cuadra Directory of Online Databases, 1991.

Growth in commercial databases 1980-1990

In purely competitive terms, no time before ours has presented so many opportunities or dangers. The recent changes in Eastern Bloc nations and the dawning of a unified Europe call for American corporations that can compete—that operate at the edge of their knowledge and capabilities. As the graph in Figure 1.2 indicates, European and Japanese companies have grown to hold a dominant position in U.S. patents in the past twenty years. Japanese firms are using our universities as a competitive tool by funding programs and research. In 1989, Germany's world exports exceeded ours, as well as those of other developed nations. Even with all its inevitable social and economic dislocations, the new united Germany will be a force to be reckoned with.

Fig. 1.2

Source: U.S. Patent & Trademark Office

**Share of U.S. patents granted
to foreign companies**

Given this changing scene, competitive intelligence is an activity of increasing importance. Whether the need is for knowledge about an industry, a market, a product or a competitor, reliable global information is central to our national success. As Frederick the Great reportedly said, "It is pardonable to be defeated, but not to be surprised." With today's information resources, and a CI program that reflects the information needs of the corporation, surprises can be minimized.

But this is a book about the process and resources of competitive intelligence, not about the electronic transformation of information itself. It may well be that the electronic manipulation and storage of information will have the effect on our times that the invention of the movable-type printing press exerted on fifteenth-century Europe. For the first time in history, books and the literate population needed to read them came together. In much the same way, access to an increasing world of information empowers the modern corporation to understand itself and its markets more completely than ever before.

Competitive intelligence definitions

We like to think of competitive intelligence as the selection, collection, interpretation and distribution of publicly-held information that has strategic importance. Needless to say, there are other definitions of competitive intelligence. Here is a sampling:

> *Business intelligence* [an alternate term for competitive intelligence] *is the activity of monitoring the environment external to the firm for information that is relevant for the decision-making process of the company.*[2]

> *Competitor intelligence is the analytical process that transforms disaggregated competitor intelligence into relevant, accurate and usable strategic knowledge about competitors' position, performance, capabilities and intentions.*[3]

> *Competitive intelligence is a way of thinking.*[4]

> *CI uses public sources to locate and develop information on competition and competitors.*[5]
>
> *Competitor intelligence is "highly specific and timely information about a corporation."*[6]
>
> *The objective of competitor intelligence is not to steal a competitor's trade secrets or other proprietary property, but rather to gather in a systematic, overt (i.e., legal) manner a wide range of information that when collated and analyzed provides a fuller understanding of a competitor firm's structure, culture, behavior, capabilities and weaknesses.*[7]

But definitions, to paraphrase Samuel Johnson, are like watches—and none is ever exactly correct. True, we do competitive intelligence openly, but we would rather the target company be kept in the dark, and that it remain so. (Surprise is no small thing in competition.) True, we usually digest, analyze and arrange the materials in our reports, but sometimes, as in a database search that lays out production figures for ten years in "report format" on a certain product, analysis and digestion may simply be gilding the lily. The heart of the matter is sometimes just in the "raw" numbers or facts. True, we may sometimes need a wide range of material on a broad span of corporate functions, but sometimes a very focused and narrow bit of information is what's required. (What kind of machinery are they using in that plant?).

Does corporate competitive intelligence bear any resemblance to the intelligence work done by the CIA, or in John le Carré novels? It is ridiculous to deny that there are similarities. To the extent that both require probing the environment for information that could hurt or help the client organization, yes, they are alike. In both cases, whether working for a corporation or for the government, the chase for information is interesting and exciting, as is getting "the goods" for the client. Both require the selection, collection, interpretation and distribution of information. But beyond this, similarities fade. Projects in CI can sometimes feel as if they were life-and-death matters, but they are not. Not really. The CIA and other government intelligence agencies have been known to work outside of the law. Corporate competitive- or business-intelligence does not operate this way.

Competitive intelligence has nothing to do with espionage! CI, as we will discuss it here, does not use illicit or illegal methods to accomplish its goals.

Some common goals of competitive intelligence:

- Detecting competitive threats
- Eliminating or lessening surprises
- Enhancing competitive advantage by lessening reaction time
- Finding new opportunities

Competitive intelligence has such a broad scope it can utilize information related to almost any product or activity, or information on recent industry trends or issues (packaging companies track changes in environmental regulations constantly), or word about geopolitical trends (e.g., today 30% of all business aircraft are sold to Pacific Basin companies). CI can be driven by something as seemingly mundane as the need for a biographical profile of a newly appointed corporate executive, or something as important as the news that a steel competitor is making major investments on R&D in ceramics and electronics. It might even be the suspicion that a future competitor in an unrelated industry will soon threaten the corporation through new technology.

A future competitor of the Royal Typewriter Company was once a couple of young men, Steve Jobs and Steve Wozniak, ingeniously soldering a collection of micro-chips, wires and a cathode-ray-tube into a sort of jungle-gym computer in their California garage. What came of this homely tinkering was the Apple Computer. Steve Jobs' and Steve Wozniak's work on the "home computer" started an industry, an industry that was to reshape the typewriter business, and a lot of other businesses as well, in profound ways over the years that followed. (Later, when IBM decided that Apple had defined a market for their PC, following Apple's lead definitively changed IBM's business.) A future technological threat to the vacuum tube was the micro-chip, and a future competitor to the buggy-whip business was Henry Ford's automobile. One question is, if they are in unrelated industries, how do you find them before it's too late?

Some of these future competitors will bob to the surface, where good management with sound competitive analysis can spot them in time, and steer around them; others will ride in like an iceberg, silent, with 90% of their mass below the waterline where it can do the most damage. In some cases, vision and the ability to see what is coming are of little use.

"Let's not worry about it, those little cars aren't what Americans want to buy," is an instance of Detroit's sight-ing the competitive iceberg back in the 1960's and not reacting for thirty years. It is quite possible that Detroit auto manufacturers will never be able to compete with the quality being built into Japanese and European cars. One commentator observed that the institutional personality of the Detroit auto manufacturers is so pervasive and strong that the only way it may be able to change its ways is to move to another part of the country. "Send a bright young person full of new ideas to Detroit and within six months he or she will be thinking and talking the party line. 'These are good American cars, and just what our customer wants.' "

Japanese camera manufacturers have recently introduced cameras utilizing magnetic media, rather than photosensitive film. ("Photographs" captured digitally are viewed on video monitors (TV), a factor slide projector manufacturers should have identified some time ago, and should have included in their systematic competitor scans, along with the products of competing slide-projector producers.) Eastman Kodak will easily be able to provide magnetic storage disks for these cameras, as will Fuji, 3M and a host of other manufacturers, but may eventually ship its slide projectors primarily to the Smithsonian, where they will be viewed only as curiosities. Eastman Kodak may or may not want to compete in video monitors—the replacement technology for the slide viewer and slide projector— against Sony, Panasonic and a host of other foreign entrenched electronics manufacturers. Much of the technology and production capacity for home electronics appears to have been lost to Japan and the Pacific Basin. Such capacity may have been permanently lost by the U.S., unless current research on digital HD (High Definition)TV gives us with new access to consumer electronics again.

Not every company, no matter how large and powerful, properly understands the nature of its own business, or its customer base. Nor does every company or division always understand or act in its own best interests. Without the vision empowered by such an understanding, no amount of CI will help forestall the inevitable. Without such an understanding, threats cannot be seen for what they are, if they can be seen at all. In important ways competitive intelligence is about exactly this; about perceiving threats, and ways of getting at the information you need once the threat is somehow perceived.

Who does competitive intelligence?

Those working in CI range from public, legal or corporate librarians and information center analysts to management personnel, specialists in financial data, business-development people and strategic planners to ex CIA operatives and retired military intelligence personnel, information specialists and academicians. (One of the authors of this book, John Moorhead, is a former U.S. Naval Intelligence Officer.) Many corporate practitioners, according to a survey done by the Conference Board, are marketing directors or marketing research managers. It seems that at this point in CI's evolutionary progress, to quote Lawrence of Arabia, "nothing is written."

Outside agencies that perform competitor intelligence work run the gamut from certain public relations firms and the consulting arms of CPA firms to young companies devoted to competitor analysis and industrial research.

Competitive intelligence has only recently emerged as a distinctive field of endeavor. Only one association, the recently-formed Society of Competitive Intelligence Professionals, now exists to serve this field directly, but a number of others, such as the Information Industry Association, the Planning Forum and perhaps even the American Marketing Association and the Special Libraries Association serve some related interests and overlapping information needs.

Every discipline, no matter how ancient or recent, has schools of thought, gurus, cherished beliefs, taboos, and so forth. Newer ones simply have less baggage. Gurus, or authors of key works, will be covered in a later chapter. The taboo against using non-legitimate information resources we've already talked about. There is also a commandment to be ethical in the pursuit of information. At the practitioner, or "schools-of-thought" level, three recognizable groups of CI specialists stand out:

The first group holds that interpretation and analysis are the essential activities in CI.
"It is clearly possible," as a professor of statistical measurement once said, "to lie with numbers, but it is much easier to lie without them." The question here is, do our tools of analysis have validity as well as reliability, and what is the device or matrix that will most easily communicate the complexities of an industry or a corporate position relative to its peer corporations? Finally, no matter how good the analysis (valid and reliable data that is communicated through the written word or displayed through graphs), unless the matter is communicated to those who need to know, the task is pointless.

The second group holds that the hunting, gathering and location of reliable information is the essential activity. The question here is how to keep abreast of the proliferation of databases and printed resources (books, magazines, newspapers, reports), and how to keep abreast of the procedures to get at non-published information. (Locating and requesting a document or a government filing requires some finesse, even when one is being open and ethical.)

A third group believes that the gathering of valid/reliable information and the analyzing of it are equally important, and that if one of these two activities is weak or impaired, the other will probably be flawed.

It's understood that raw information or "data dumps" have limited usefulness, and are not usually a product that is given to the client. Data and nearly any type of information usually needs to be integrated and analyzed into a document that is well organized and that can easily be read and interpreted. Graphs, tables and charts are often useful communication aids.

At the same time, if one does not know the kinds of information that can be found during the hunting and gathering process—either electronically or in hard copy— one cannot ask the right questions. For example, PIERS, a Journal of Commerce database (begun over 100 years ago) with import/export data now available via the DIALOG database gateway service, allows the researcher to track the movement of export/import materials from one company location to another company location abroad. Only knowing about this resource would lead a manager to ask, (in a legitimate, legal world) "what products or materials have been shipped to X company in the past year?"

If management can't be expected to ask the right questions about the competitive environment without understanding the forms of information that shape that environment, what does this mean to CI?

It means campaigns and programs to inform and educate management—a corporate management that has taken the right first step in setting up a CI function, but who now need to understand what kinds of information can be found. Without such proselytizing, at minimum, competitive intelligence will be underutilized; at worst the CI program will die an untimely and unwarranted death.

[1] Robert Glynn Kelly, **A Lament for Barney Stone**, New York, Holt, Rinehart Winston, 1961.

[2] Benjamin and Tamar Gilad, **The Business Intelligence System** ... New York, AMACOM, 1988, p. viii.

[3] Seminar guide, **The Competitor Intelligence Group**, division of Kirk Tyson Associates, Ltd., 1986, p. III-11.

[4] William Rothschild, **How to Gain (and Maintain) the Competitive Advantage in Business**, New York, McGraw Hill, 1984, p. 179.

[5] John J. McGonagle, Jr. and Carolyn M. Vella, **Outsmarting the Competition**, Naperville, IL, Sourcebooks, 1990, p. viii.

[6] Leonard Fuld, **Competitor Intelligence: How to Get It; How to Use It**, New York, John Wiley & Sons, 1985, p. 5.

[7] William L. Sammon, et al., **Business Competitor Intelligence**, New York, John Wiley & Sons, 1985, p. 62.

Axioms of
competitive intelligence

Most of the information needed for a given project is available through publicly available channels.
The percentage most practitioners place on this kind of public information varies from 80% to 90%. Given the amount of information available in our age, this 80% to 90%, if analyzed and presented carefully, can be more than adequate for most needs. The last 10% is insignificant.

Information is where you find it.
This caveat simply means that while you may have your cherished sources and resources for certain kinds of information, vital information is often found in unlikely places. We once found sales and profit numbers for a large privately held company that were included in the transcript of an Environmental Protection Agency hearing. The company was trying to show that it couldn't afford a large EPA fine, and in doing so had sent its CFO to testify at the hearing. He brought along his spreadsheets for the prior three years, which became part of the hearing, and subsequently became a matter of public record through the minutes of the hearing.

CI projects pass through phases that are best described with a U-shaped curve.
At the beginning of the project the researcher is filled with optimism about accomplishing it. Soon after actually starting to research the project the researcher's enthusiasm bottoms out and he or she feels the material to complete the project successfully will not materialize. Time passes and data and information begins to accumulate, and as the project takes shape the researcher starts up the far side of the curve.

Someone else cares about the subject.
No matter how small, obscure or esoteric the subject, it is
undoubtedly of interest to someone besides yourself and
your client. This someone may be a newspaper editor in a
small town where the company is located, or it may be the
editor of a specialty newsletter, or an industry specialist in
government, or a competitor of the company you are
scanning, or a distributor of the product, or a warehouse
manager, or the head of an association. In one case involving production of a speciality material so small it wasn't
tracked by the usual sources, the investigating firm located
the man who had invented the product twenty years ago
when he worked for a large multi-national corporation. He
had been running his own business for fifteen years, but
had developed his own sources for keeping track of his
brainchild. The investigation had led to someone who was
interested.

Single sources of information are unreliable.
Information gleaned from one source of information may
be absolutely correct, but again it may not be. It is, on the
face of it, unreliable for the purposes of competitive intelligence. In CI work the primary use for information from a
single source is as something to be confirmed by a second
source. Corroborated information from two or more
sources is probably reliable. Information that cannot be
corroborated must be treated as a rumor. It may still have
its uses to the client, who may think the rumor is as good
as gold, and it may be. But if it is just a rumor and it is
presented as a fact, your professional judgment may be
called into question.

Real market share is harder to find than it would appear to be.

This wouldn't matter if clients weren't trying to find it so eagerly, but it does, because they are. Part of the problem is that share of market is often sought for small privately-held companies or divisions of large privately-held companies, where only the CEO and two other people may know the answer during certain times of the year. Part of the problem is the unknowability of total market size for smaller industries. Part of the problem is dissimilarity of product lines, even in large companies, so that even two companies that seem to be making the same product often aren't. Product line and share is also complicated by the way SIC numbers (Standard Industrial Classification codes that are used to categorize industries) are used by manufacturers and others. Also, companies tend to be identified by SIC numbers in three or four digits, rather than out to the more precise seven or eight digits. Use of four-digit codes amplifies the imprecise nature of the SIC numbers themselves. Some hard-copy sources, such as directories, limit their market-share lists to publicly-held corporations, which nearly always distorts the picture of the market and the key players. A number of information products—including the recently-acquired TriNet database—propose to display market-share for their readers or searchers, but regrettably, it doesn't usually happen in such a way that is usable. If the market is small enough, no one may have bothered to break it out, and it may have to be built laboriously brick-by-brick. Building market size and market share information in this way can take months, and involve interviews with a considerable number of industry participants.

Companies, like individuals, leave a paper trail as they go about their business.

For every action there is a reaction. If a company wishes to produce a new material involving the use of different chemicals, it will need to file with a number of regulatory agencies. Such a filing is a public document. If a company wants to expand its plant, it must file for building permits, and these too become public documents. Later, when such corporate agents as construction engineers and architects file their supporting documents and blueprints for the plant expansion, these become public documents as well.

The job of CI is to understand the corporate world well enough to find the paper that company actions generate.

Public information

Lo! I had made a public thoroughfare of the sanctuary of my mind.

St. Thomas Deciduous, 604-656 A.D.[8]

We've said that competitive intelligence utilizes public information. Public in this sense simply means information that can be somehow got at legitimately. This distinction is near to being a core concept within CI, because it helps define what is ethical or permissible behavior.

> **Pub-lish** 1 a: to make generally known b: to make public announcement of ... 3 a: to place before the public b: to produce or release for publication.
>
> **Pub-lic** 5 a: accessible to or shared by all members of the community.
> **Webster's 7th New Collegiate Dictionary**

This does not mean that public information is something a company might want to have known to outsiders. It's just that corporations leave a paper trail as they go about their business. Corporations take some pains to insure that their strategic planning and product-release agenda remains confidential. In almost every case, the timing of a particular strategic action is important, and the foreknowledge of this action by competitors is undesirable. In more volatile industries, timing may be critical to the success of the product. A me-too product can often be introduced quickly, stealing precious market-share, or worse yet, a competitor's superior product may be released before yours is rolled out, if your planning becomes public knowledge.

"Ideally, any time you can dramatically improve an existing technology,... you should have a breakthrough product that makes you the dominant force in the marketplace. But a fast-moving competitor with a better understanding of the market and an ability to match your technological ingenuity may succeed in paving the path to his door more quickly."[9]

Sony was there first with a VCR in its proprietary "Beta" format. But a smaller competitor, JVC, came up with a similar technology a few months later with a different format of its own invention called VHS, and solicited the cooperation of a number of other Japanese electronics firms to help in its manufacture and marketing. As we know, JVC now rules the market-place, and with a quality of video output somewhat less exacting than Sony's.

Corporations are not always internally consistent or coordinated in their efforts to keep their perceived secrets to themselves.

> The Dutch electronics company Philips is one
> of the last companies in Europe to continue
> fighting the Japanese in the mass market for
> home electronics.... Philips' video factory in
> Vienna is as modern and automated as most
> in Japan. When asked for information about
> production techniques, Philips corporate
> public relations office in London refused,
> saying this was "strategic information." Later,
> when showing visitors around the factory,
> Philips' managers proudly revealed every-
> thing that the British office had wanted to
> keep secret.[10]

The varieties of publicly-available information are too numerous to detail. But as we've mentioned, 80-90% of the information a project requires can usually be found through publicly available channels, and the rest often can be deduced or estimated. The trick is in knowing which channels are likely to be productive, and which might have only limited information. Given the realities of time and financial constraints, it is important to spend finite project resources on the most productive areas.

We said at the outset that CI involves locating and analyzing public information. But public information shouldn't be confused with published information. A great deal of the public but unpublished information in the world exists as filings, hearings and documents with governmental agencies and regulatory bodies. These agencies are behind every imaginable institutional doorway, ranging from the Environmental Protection Agency (EPA) branch in a state capital, and the local labor union division, to the city-manager's office or the building permit office in a small town about to host a competitor's new production facility.

If a competitor's new plant is being built near or on wetlands, every agency from the EPA to the Army Corps of Engineers will have to pass on the acceptability of the site. (Even new construction built on a conventional site requires applications to a score of local, state and federal agencies.) To approve or disapprove the site each agency will require from the manufacturer such documents as blueprints, projections of vehicle/truck traffic, plans to handle waste disposal, descriptions of materials to be used in manufacturing, employment projections, electrical energy use projections, descriptions of equipment to be used in the manufacturing process, and the building budget and building program. Each of these agencies, with all of its documents, is a potential information resource through something as formal as a request filed under the Freedom of Information Act (which makes government documents available under certain conditions), or through something as simple as a business-like but pleasant verbal request.

Company directories are good sources of basic information about location, sales, number of employees, management, and other core facts. Examples include Dun's **Million Dollar Directory** and Standard & Poor's **Register of Corporations, Directors and Executives**. Dun's also has a directory of overseas corporations. **The Directory of Corporate Affiliations** is a good source for tracking "who owns whom."

Other kinds of directories are useful, too. **The Encyclopedia of Associations** is invaluable in finding knowledgeable trade sources, for example.

Government filings come in all shapes and sizes, from an exhaustively detailed 10K to a state corporate registration with only the name, address and registered agent of the company. But these filings hold much usually reliable information. Some commercial databases specialize in government filings, such as Information America which provides Secretary of State and UCC information on line. In California, real estate transactions are available online.

Of course, all information on commercial databases and gateways or vendors one searches such as DIALOG, DOW

JONES, NEWSNET, NEXIS and DATASTAR will be public *and* published by definition. Full-text databases of local or regional newspapers, such as VU/TEXT or DATATIMES, can be extremely useful not just for their coverage, but also for sources to contact.

Now and then, when no local newspaper is available online, we have gone to a local newspaper publisher or to a local public library. In a recent project we got the name of a distributor we'd been looking for this way. And we learned that a new facility was built to allow the company to double its output without further construction, that the company would be expanding into new product lines, that a generic product carried a trade name we did not know about, and a few other choice tidbits. All this came from two small articles rounded up for us by a public librarian who kept a clipping file about local businesses. He mailed them to us, along with a modest bill for the copying charges.

Individual types of public information—government documents, database retrieval, corporate directories, interviews and other sources—are discussed more fully in later chapters.

The world is filled with other legitimate public information that is available, but simply less accessible than published material. The table on the following page shows a sampling of some less accessible public information resources.

Public information resources

Resource Available	Types of Documents/ Information Available
Regulatory agencies	- Plans and blueprints, project costs, etc. - Financial date - Profitability
Newspaper articles	- Executive interviews - Plant openings - Company profiles
Newspaper reporters	- Background on an article - Extra information not included in article
U. S. industrial experts	- Volume of sales for certain products - Domestic vs. import/ export production - Near-term industrial outlook
Trade associations	- Industry/product information - List of companies within an industry

8   Robert Glynn Kelly, **A Lament for Barney Stone,** New York, Holt Rinehart Winston, 1961, p. 62.
9   P. Ranganath Nayak & John M. Ketteringham, **Breakthroughs!** New York, Rawston Associates, 1986, p. 15-16.
10   "Crossed lines at Philips," *New Scientist,* Sept. 29, 1990, p. 13.

The international
background of CI

Hardly any time has been as important to the American corporation as the decade we have just entered. Foreign companies, both Japanese and European, have made inroads into domestic market share across a bridge of industries ranging from steel and automotive to home electronics and ceramics. In some cases, entire industries and their infrastructure have been abandoned to foreign competition. Foreign student SAT scores exceed those of U.S. students dramatically, with grave implications for our future technological capability. (A German firm we know of was unable to sell its packaging machine to U.S. bottlers because management felt the control panel was too complex for their under-educated work-force. It did not seem to matter that the machine offered economies of production and efficiency—economies which would have offset the cost of training operators by a significant degree. Turning away from enhanced productivity by saying "our workers aren't educated or literate enough to handle that" has become an expensive mind-set.)

Both European and Far Eastern companies commonly expend far more than their U.S. counterparts on research (see Fig. 4.1). Sad to say, our products still may not, in spite of some efforts to change and improve, have a level of quality to match those of many European or Japanese companies. Many of our large firms are top-heavy, compared to their international competition, with layers of management between the worker and the CEO undreamt of elsewhere in the developed world. A major business news publication recently foresaw the era of the nineties as a "competitive hell" for the U.S. corporation. It may very well prove to be exactly that, particularly if we continue to conduct our domestic business as we have done in recent decades.

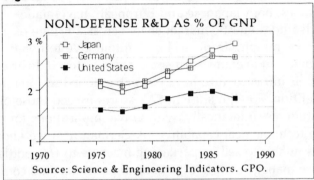

Source: Science & Engineering Indicators. GPO.

U.S. vs. Japanese research spending

The Boston Consulting Group, along with the *Wall Street Journal*, recently polled Japanese and American managers on the need for "more R&D spending within their companies." Ninety-seven percent of the Japanese managers saw a need for greater research and development expenditures in their corporations, compared with sixty-one percent among U.S. managers.

Without the advantages accruing from major and steady R&D investment, U.S. companies may find themselves in the situation of some underdeveloped nations: rich in natural resources, but unable to bring those resources to market by adding value to them.

According to Jonathan Aylen, who periodically surveys the world steel industry, Japanese-owned steel mills are investing major R&D resources into such non-steel areas as ceramics and electronics. *Aylen noted in* **Research-Technology Management** *that one company, Nippon Steel, is spending more on research than all eight leading U.S. mills combined.*[11] He noted that European Community R&D steel investment is on a par with Japan's. Aylen has a regular column in the **Steel Times International**.

Japanese corporations use our elite universities as a key resource in science and technology research. Everywhere leading-edge research is happening, from Stanford and Harvard to MIT, Japanese corporations are actively funding and endowing research. Half of the foreign companies participating in MIT's Industrial Liaison Program are Japanese. In addition to this, over a third of the corporate chairs endowed at MIT are sponsored by Japanese companies. These 19 chairs represent some $20 million to MIT. Evan Herbert has taken a look at the Japanese use of American technology and information, and it is a foreboding picture in some ways. [12]

Academia insists that it does not sell its services, but rather seeks sponsors, and this is a "sponsorship" aggressive Japanese technology-driven companies are happy to provide. What do such companies get for their dollar? The keys to the store.

Fujitsu Limited, Japan's chief computer manufacturer, endowed the MIT Fujitsu Professorship of Electrical Engineering and Computer Science for $1.5 million in 1988. MIT chose one of its most respected scholars, Robert G. Gallager, to fill this chair. Gallager authored **Information Theory and Reliable Communication**. He co-directs the Laboratory for Information and Decision Systems, was President of the Information Theory Society in 1971, and is recognized for his work in flow control, data compression and routing. What else does Fujitsu get for its $1.5 million? Access to MIT's other resources, primarily.

Marvin Minsky, arguably the leading authority on artificial intelligence, is also on the faculty at MIT. Minsky is one of two people Isaac Asimov named when asked if he knew someone smarter than he was. (The other was the astronomer and author, Carl Sagan.) How could Japan resist having access to such talent? Why should anyone expect them to resist?

In its promotional literature, MIT notes: "The Industrial Liaison Program places at your disposal the expertise and resources of all the schools, departments, centers and laboratories of MIT." Given the value received, $1.5 million dollars just sounds like smart shopping.

Recent changes in the status of Eastern Bloc nations and the ongoing evolution of the Economic Community do nothing to lessen this competitive threat. Given these events, and our recent failure to compete across a spectrum of technological areas, it behooves the American corporation to go through an agonizing reappraisal of its strategic position. The reasons for diminished competitive vigor probably have less to do with ability than with mindset and attitude, but whatever the reasons, surely a knowledge of the competitive environment and the resources that define it is a necessary prelude to change.

A competitive parable:
The snail and the predatory crayfish

> The growth patterns of a snail called *Physella*
> *virgata virgata* are significantly altered by the
> presence of a certain predatory crayfish. In an
> environment relatively free of this predatory
> crayfish, the snail reproduces when its shell is
> about 4 millimeters in length. The life span of
> snails in this environment is some three to
> five months (*Science Magazine*). However, if
> the water is also inhabited by the *Orconectes*
> *virilis* crayfish, the snails grow to twice their
> normal size, live over twice as long (11 to 14
> months), and reproduce later. Scientists
> studying this phenomenon hypothesize that
> in such a harsh environment, the snail reallo-
> cates its resources away from reproduction
> and toward growth and community survival.

Suppose we compare this genetic developmental/biologi-
cal response to the industrial/competitive environment
that the European Economic Community and the changes
in Eastern Bloc nations will undoubtedly foster. This was
the environment Europe and Japan struggled with following WWII, when immediate pleasures had to be postponed
for growth and community survival. (An analogy to "early
reproduction" for U.S. corporations might be our short-
sighted focus on quarterly or annual "results" rather than
managing resources for long-term benefit.)

Michael Porter, writing of the research findings in his
recent book, **The Competitive Advantage of Nations**,
noted: "... I found that competitive advantage springs not
from static inefficiencies but from improvement,

innovation and the ability relentlessly to upgrade competitive advantages to more sophisticated types. *These in turn result not from a comfortable home environment but from pressure and challenge.*"[13]

We could have used a few more predatory "crayfish" in our comfortable home environment, apparently, and a bit more pressure and challenge. As William Shakespeare wrote, *Sweet are the uses of adversity; Which like the toad, ugly and venomous, Wears yet a precious jewel in his head;...*[14]

11   Jonathan Aylen, "Japanese Firms Diversify R&D," *Research-Technology   Management,* Jan.-Feb., 1990, p. 4.

12   Evan Herbert, "Japanese R&D in the United States," in *Research-Technology Management,* December, 1989.

13   Michael Porter, "Don't Collaborate, Compete," *The Economist,* June 9, 1990.

14   William Shakespeare, **As You Like It**, Act II, Sc. I, Line 12.

Competitive intelligence books

All of the books in this chapter cover the rules and strategies of competitive intelligence, but most recognize that getting at the information is only the start of a process of piecing together clues to find out something. Seldom is what you want to know just handed to you: "Yes, this is what is happening and here are the statistics to back it up." Usually it's a jigsaw puzzle you have to put together because nobody else bothered to put it together before, or because, even though the information is available to the public, some people don't want the public to figure it out.

Finding the right sources is often a trial-and-error activity. It is hard to automate because projects are so different. Yes, you would think there would only be a few different kinds of projects for a competitive intelligence researcher to work on. Sure, "no-brainers" like retrieving the financial statements of public companies will provide a relaxing interlude where you can be master of all you survey. But all you survey usually includes a fair number of tough questions.

Even the best of the books only get you started on the road to solving the tough ones. One of the problems is that competitive intelligence is still a young concept. No consensus says what it is. So books about competitive intelligence are like the old story about the blindfolded counselors who are asked to describe an elephant. They pat it in various places and decide that it is a tube, or a spear, or a leathery mass. There are writers who portray competitive intelligence as the act of consulting certain sources, traditional like reading magazine articles or inventive like counting cars in a company parking lot. There are writers who see competitive intelligence as a team effort, the corporation working together to get smarter. And there are those writers who see competitive intelligence as a quest, an adventure.

None, however, can rightfully call it spying; people who write about competitive intelligence are careful to make the point that it is not James Bond stuff or industrial espionage. Competitive intelligence is whatever you need to do to understand something that is important for you— and your business. But that does not include doing illegal or unethical things—such practices break the rules of the game. Also, they are not necessary, even beside the point. Competitive intelligence is about what companies do in markets, and markets by their very nature (unless they are black or very small) are open, public affairs. The game is to understand what is happening well enough to be on the cutting edge of competitiveness in those markets.

Now, what do the books tell you? Here is one message:

Competitive intelligence is important, especially now when economic life in the United States is getting tougher.
One writer, Ian Gordon, says CI is important because nowadays markets are a zero sum game: you have to take market share away from someone else to grow. The Japanese know that. They have been concentrating on competitive intelligence for a long time. That is one of the few ways to get an edge when your economy has been totally destroyed and you have nothing to build with but your wits (and American aid, of course).

Yet what competitive intelligence actually is, and how to practice it, is much more murky. Some of these books barely mention sources of information. They simply ignore the issue. Other books lay out extensive sources of information, and give the larger issues short shrift. Some books are cheerleaders; others are teachers; and still others are books of lists. Each approach has its uses and merits. One of the exciting things about competitive intelligence right now is the way it is changing and growing. Today's practitioners are present at the creation.

Here are some approaches to competitive intelligence that these books suggest. Read any two or three of the standard books on CI and you will recognize these descriptions:

One approach is to lay out recommended sources and give advice on how to use them.
Information is where you find it, right? And the more places you look, the better. Usually these sources are published information, or public information that is not published (any information available to the public, or disclosed to the public, that is not yet published, including interviews), or government filings.

Lists of sources can jog your memory as to a source you might not be aware of. One problem with source lists in books like this, however, is that they can become quickly out of date, especially if addresses and telephone numbers are provided. Frequently updated directories, of which there are many, are usually the best place to find these kinds of referrals. However, in general terms, it is important to know what is available and how to find it. These books provide that service.

Another approach is to look at CI from a theoretical perspective.
What is CI good for? How does it contribute to the success of a business organization? Why is intelligence important? This approach produces the best writing on competitive intelligence, and gets closest to the essence of the task. For all the source lists, for all the guidance on how to set up a competitive intelligence function in-house, the task is to perceive and communicate insights to those who can use them. Several CI books issue the important warning against collecting too much miscellaneous information. The aim is to collect only the information you need, not to create huge files that will seldom if ever be accessed.

The middle road between the listing of sources and the theoretical overview combines both to give guidance on why and how to conduct CI.
All the books on CI attempt in some degree to reach this golden mean. None of them do, including the book you hold in your hands. The reason is that CI is highly situational. All the guidance, all the source lists in the world, important as they are, will not get the individual job done. It takes an analyst with the curiosity and persistence, along with the resources, to work through a question to get an answer that managers can use. Because CI is time sensitive, the answer is often based on temporary conditions that need to be identified and analyzed under a deadline. Books can provide the tools, but analysts must use them.

That said, what follows then is a sampling–hopefully a representative one–of the literature of competitive intelligence, ranging from the esoteric to the practical, from Michael Porter's theoretical analyses to **Washington Researchers** books of lists.

Berkman, Robert I.
Find It Fast: How to uncover information on any subject
New York, NY: Harper & Row
1987, 1990

This useful guide discusses information resources and research strategies in clear, user-friendly prose. It takes an excellent, clear-minded approach to the research process. Hard-copy as well as database sources are covered, and it is especially cogent in showing how to contact and interview experts. This is a good basic text which incidentally is enjoyable to read.

Fifer, Robert M.; Furey, Timothy R.; Pryor, Lawrence S.; and Rumburg, Jeffrey P.
Beating the Competition: A practical guide to bench-marking
Vienna,VA: Kaiser Associates, Inc., 1988

"Benchmarking" refers to comparing your company to a competitor, by a single function (for instance, packaging), by several functions, or across the board. The activity has a heavy CI component, because to compare yourself in detail to other companies, you must first assemble detailed information about those other companies. This is a clear and readable guide to the process.

Fuld, Leonard M.
Competitor Intelligence: How to get it; how to use it
New York, NY: John Wiley & Sons
1985

Leonard Fuld is one of the pioneers of competitive intelligence research. His combination of traditional and innovative competitive intelligence techniques is one model upon which competitive intelligence practitioners have based their activities. This, his first book, gives general guidance and a considerable amount of advice and detail on specific sources of intelligence information. The book includes "war stories" from actual competitive intelligence projects to illustrate his points.

Fuld, Leonard M.
Monitoring the Competition: Find out what's really going on over there
New York, NY: John Wiley & Sons
1988

This second book by Leonard Fuld is more user-friendly than his first book, though less detailed. It takes the reader by the hand on a walk through the CI process. The guidance is clear and sound. Examples, set off graphically from the text, give the book life and illustrate important points. The book is a good short guide to the CI process.

Gilad, Benjamin and Gilad, Tamar
The Business Intelligence System
New York, NY: AMACOM (American Management Association)
1988

This concise and detailed book gives a well-textured guide to planning, setting up and operating an effective business intelligence system within an organization. The guidance is sensible, and well bolstered with examples from the authors' experience with actual companies and their intelligence efforts. The book is especially good in explaining how to create an internal intelligence collection and analysis function, so that it functions over the long term and makes real contributions to the organization. As an example of the Gilads' prose, here is an excellent summation of the nature and sources of business intelligence (BI) from the book's first chapter: "BI concerns the *ethical* gathering and use of publicly and semipublicly available information as a basis for planning. Publicly available information refers mainly to published data to which the public has access. Semipublic information refers to data obtained from the field, such as information from customers, suppliers, peers, and others."

Gordon, Ian
Beat the Competition!: How to use competitive intelligence to develop winning business strategies
Oxford, UK: Basil Blackwell Ltd.
1989

Gordon presents a fulsome and interesting discussion of how competitive intelligence fits into the wider field of business strategy. It argues for the importance of competitive information and monitoring at a time when economic

growth is not vigorous and most markets are mature. The
book gives detailed and sensible guidance on how 'to go
about setting up a competitive intelligence function and
how to use CI to inform business strategy. For instance,
Gordon discusses shadow marketing as an effective way to
approach the CI process. Shadow marketing involves
having a staff member "become" the CEO of a competitor
company and try to think like that competitor, using
whatever information is available. The writing style is
clear, although occasionally jargon intrudes.

Mathey, Charles J.
Competitive Analysis
New York, NY: American Management Association
1991

This monograph, written for top-level managers, was
provided to us in pre-publication draft form. The writer
shares a detailed understanding of the collection and
analytical options available to a CI researcher, and the
trade-offs among these options. He also emphasizes his
belief that CI is more than nice-to-know information. It
contributes directly to the corporate bottom line. "The fact
is, based on personal observations," he argues, "competitive analysis has a higher ROI [return on investment] than
R&D at most companies. The amount of investment is
small, and the payoff is big when the right questions are
asked." Mathey approaches his subject as a consultant
helping an organization implement a competitive intelligence project or program.

This monograph explains techniques and options used by
the competitive analyst, so that managers can understand

where the information comes from and how it is produced. Mr. Mathey argues persuasively that "the essence of any competitive analysis activity is that it contributes to making better and faster decisions. Thus, a competitive analysis activity should not be undertaken unless the use of the results is clear."

His focus on analysis is welcome. Excellent books exist on other phases of the business intelligence process (collection of information and organizing a competitive intelligence function within a corporation), but the specifics of analysis have received relatively little attention.

The attention they get here is helpful, if a little idiosyncratic. Mr. Mathey spends considerable time in the middle chapters on how competitive strategies are pursued (as opposed to how they are analyzed). He discusses how to discourage competitors from entering a market or to carve out a bigger market share. Strategies such as low price and high quality are discussed, and interesting examples are given. Product concepts that did not quite make it, like wrist-twist steering for Fords and a Hoover automatic floor washer, are described (neither product found a wide market because they were too different for consumers to accept readily).

The reader is well into the book before reaching specific analysis techniques. Once there, Mr. Mathey discusses the importance of reading published material, studying government filings such as SEC documents, and interviewing experts (including Delphi studies and conferences).

After information has been gleaned from these sources, Mr. Mathey advocates sorting the information by corporate function (manufacturing, engineering, marketing, etc.). Then the information can be reoriented or distilled in a number of ways.

A matrix is provided which shows costs, benefits, skills requirements, and applicability of analysis techniques. A helpful glossary of terms also is included.

This is a useful book which provides information not available elsewhere and some highly readable insights into competitive dynamics in U. S. corporations.

McGonagle, John J., and Vella, Carolyn M.
Outsmarting the Competition: Practical approaches to finding and using competitive information
Naperville, IL: Sourcebooks, Inc.
1990

This book goes over the basics of competitive intelligence practice. It provides competitive intelligence information with much the same approach as Fuld: This is how you do it, and this is what you use to do it. In a subject where a significant body of literature is just beginning to form, different perspectives are especially valuable, and this book comes at the issues from a slightly different angle. It has a good texture of examples, and its approach is down-to-earth practical. In fact, the authors occasionally explain too much, and get too basic. Nevertheless, this is a useful practitioner's handbook.

Meyer, Herbert E.
Real-World Intelligence: Organized information for executives
New York, NY: Weidenfeld & Nicolson
1987

The best written of the current books on competitive intelligence, this small volume gives a useful overview of the business intelligence process. It tells why business intelligence is important, demystifies it, describes it as a means of understanding the business environment and not an attempt to steal competitor secrets. In fact, competitor secrets are really beside the point, unimportant when compared to the effort to understand and cope with the competitive environment. This understanding does not come easily but it is reachable with public information alone, Meyer argues.

Porter, Michael E.
Competitive Strategy: Techniques for analyzing industries and competitors
New York, NY: The Free Press/Macmillan
1980

Competitive Advantage: Creating and sustaining superior performance
New York, NY: The Free Press/Macmillan
1985

Michael Porter is the "present at the creation" writer on competitive intelligence. His two books considered here, **Competitive Strategy** and **Competitive Advantage**, are studied by business school students as well as active managers. Porter has a specific and well-thought-out view of how industries and companies work. He also believes in

qualitative information (separate from "number crunching") as a powerful tool for making successful business
decisions.

Porter's books launched the current focus on competitive
intelligence as a concept and an activity. These two books
contain the core of his doctrine, although he has written
others as well. He pulls together within a theoretical
framework basic ideas and activities, practiced by many
before he wrote, to present a unified view of competitive
strategy. The books are readable, and strengthened by
well-placed examples. They emphasize the importance of
information in competitive strategy, while pointing out
that most of the information needed is available in public
sources (not secrets that have to be ferreted out by dubious
means).

His coherent view of how growing, mature and declining
businesses really work, coupled with his conviction that
these processes can be successfully managed using information, makes a heady brew. It also has fueled the establishment and growth of competitive intelligence as a
distinct discipline and a coveted niche in the corporate
hierarchy.

Prescott, John E., Editor
Advances in Competitive Intelligence
Vienna, VA: Society of Competitor Intelligence
Professionals
1989

This is basically a book of readings on competitive intelligence, divided into five sections:

> *The Evolving Field of Competitive Intelligence*
> *Case Studies of Competitive Intelligence Programs*
> *Case Applications of Competitive Intelligence Tools*
> *Techniques for Assessing Competitive Positions*
> *Continuing Challenges in Competitive Intelligence*

The readings vary in focus from this-is-how-we-do-it-here to stirring calls for creative thinking to conceptual guidance on building competitive intelligence systems. The editor has selected authors from a broad range of perspectives: academics, staff practitioners, and consultants. Editor John Prescott gets the first and last word, beginning the book with a good overview of CI components, and then ending with the results of a survey profiling competitive intelligence workers. In another article, Vincent P. Barabba has some interesting comments about creative thinking, quoting advertising executive David Ogilvy and others, and advocating an "inquiry center" to focus the thinking of the corporation. Thomas W. Leigh takes us step-by-step through a competitive analysis of the "economy lodging segment" (budget motels and hotels). Robert A. Margulies and André G. Gib describe Douglas Aircraft's ups and downs in building a competitive intelligence program that top managers wanted to use. Benjamin and Tamar Gilad discuss the "intelligence audit," in which an organization decides what it needs to know, what it already knows, and what tools it must use to find out the rest. Other articles are useful as well.

Sammon, William; Kurland, Mark; Spitalnic, Robert (and others)
Business Competitor Intelligence: Methods for collecting, organizing and using information
New York, NY: John Wiley and Sons
1984

This collection of readings, written at a management theory level, has been an influential text for CI professionals as they developed ideas of what their discipline should be. It is somewhat old now (1984), but, like Porter's books, it provides basic, bedrock guidance on the practice of CI. In the book's first article, "Competitor intelligence: The sine qua non of corporate strategic planning," James R. Gardner, director of corporate planning at Pfizer, urges a higher level of strategic planning which requires strong input of competitive intelligence. This is necessary, he says in the article's conclusion, because the days of strong market growth are over for many U. S. companies. "With softer markets comes intensified competition, companies eagerly eyeing each others' sales volume and customers to ensure their survival," Mr. Gardner argues. *"The law of the jungle has resurfaced, and those companies which do not anticipate and effectively plan for increasingly tough competition will become legitimate prey in the marketplace"* [his italics]. After Mr. Gardner's keynote, the book goes on to deal with a useful range of topics, among them "Strategic intelligence: An analytical resource for decision-makers," "Competitor intelligence in consumer industries," "The financial dimension: Penetrating the financial statements," "Media: The double-edged sword," "Legal implications of competitive intelligence," "Competitor analysis and risk assessment in a foreign environment," and "The use of competitor intelligence in acquisitions and divestments."

Stanat, Ruth
The Intelligent Corporation: Creating a shared network
for information and profit
New York, NY: AMACOM (American Management
Association)
1990

Ruth Stanat is most concerned with making an intelligence
system work within a corporation, and creating a com-
puter-based system as the vehicle for this intelligence
system. From this perspective, she looks at where the
information comes from, what needs to happen to it, and
where it goes. The aim is to create systems that decision
makers really use, systems that work for them, that suit
their purposes. She sees corporate intelligence systems
evolving through four phases:

I.   Corporate awareness of the need.

II. Establishment of a centralized information
     collection and analysis department.

III. Development of an electronic system to
     support the intelligence process.

IV. Development of a global electronic network
     linking all departments in the inward and
     outward flow of intelligence information.

Tyson, Kirk W. M.
Competitor Intelligence Manual and Guide: Gathering,
analyzing and using business intelligence
Englewood Cliffs, NJ: Prentice Hall
1990

This book is well named "manual," because it takes a
practical, hands-on approach to the competitive intelligence problem. It contains worksheets that can be used as

is or adapted to an individual function. In fact, one of Mr. Tyson's employees told us that the staff regularly photocopies the forms right out of the book for their own projects. "Isn't it great?" she said of the book. Even given her bias, "great" is a little strong for this book. "Useful" fits, though.

What really we have here is a workbook. Though not high on theory, this manual does provide a structure and the tools to implement it. The worksheets are valuable, and also the long lists of resources. In fact, sometimes the worksheets and lists of resources seem to overwhelm the descriptive text.

Tyson, Kirk W. M.
Business Intelligence: Putting it all together
Lombard, IL: Leading Edge Publications
1986

This earlier Kirk Tyson book provides advice on setting up an in-house competitor intelligence function, including lists of resources, case studies, and guides for essential tasks such as telephone interviews. The lists and tables that punctuate the book give it a "padded" feel, especially since some of the material will seem obvious to many readers. Yet it does give useful guidance and shows how CI might fit into the overall strategic planning process.

Vella, Carolyn M.
**Improved Business Planning Using Competitive
Intelligence**
Westport, CT: Greenwood Press
1988

This is a workmanlike discussion of information collection
and analysis, somewhat duplicative of Ms Vella's book
written with John McGonagle (see previous entry). This
book has its own flow and style, and its own independent
value, however. Though occasionally a bit too basic, it
takes a sensible and desmystified approach to the process,
contains some instructive examples/case studies, and
makes some points with strong clarity. One example of her
writing: "The tools of CI are relatively simple. They include computerized data bases, directories, and the telephone. But most important they include the mind." This
leaves out a company's internal information network
(formal or informal) and some hard-copy resources. But in
the overall shape it gives to the process, it is right on
target.

Washington Researchers series on Competitive Intelligence
How to Find Information About Companies: The corpo-
rate intelligence source book, Vols. 1 and 2
Company Information: A model investigation
Washington, DC: Washington Researchers
Dates vary

Washington Researchers publishes some forty guides and
two newsletters in the general area of competitive intelligence. Two of the most helpful are listed above. **How to
Find Information About Companies** is a good handbook
for both the beginner and the experienced researcher; it is
especially helpful in locating sources. **Company Informa-**

tion describes the process of researching a company with an actual example: building a case study of chicken-producer Perdue Farms Inc., whose president Frank Perdue has been so prominent in television commercials. Other titles include: **How to Find Information About Private Companies, How to Find Information About Divisions, Subsidiaries and Products,** and **Developing Industry Strategies**: A Practical Guide to Industry Analysis.

The books:

Berkman, Robert, **Find It Fast**, Harper & Row, 1990

Fifer, Robert et al., **Beating the Competition**, Kaiser Associates, 1988

Fuld, Leonard, **Competitor Intelligence**, John Wiley & Sons, 1985

Fuld, Leonard, **Monitoring the Competition**, John Wiley & Sons, 1988

Gilad, Benjamin & Tamar, **The Business Intelligence System**, AMACOM, 1988

Gordon, Ian, **Beat the Competition!**, Basil Blackwell Ltd., 1989

McGonagle, John J. Jr. and Carolyn M. Vella, **Outsmarting the Competition**, Sourcebooks, Inc., 1990

Mathey, Charles, **Competitive Analysis**, AMA, 1991

Meyer, Herbert E., **Real-World Intelligence**, Weidenfeld & Nicolson, 1987

Porter, Michael, **Competitive Strategy**, The Free Press/Macmillan, 1980

Porter, Michael, **Competitive Advantage**, The Free Press/Macmillan, 1985

Prescott, John, **Advances in Competitive Intelligence**, SCIP, 1989

Sammon, William, **Business Competitor Intelligence**, John Wiley, 1984

Stanat, Ruth, **The Intelligent Corporation**, AMACOM, 1990

Tyson, Kirk, **Business Intelligence**, Leading Edge, 1986

Tyson, Kirk, **Competitor Intelligence Manual and Guide**, Prentice Hall, 1990

Vella, Carolyn, **Improved Business Planning Using Competitive Intelligence**, Greenwood Press, 1988

Washington Researchers series on Competitive Intelligence, **How to Find Information About Companies**, and **Company Information**, Washington Researchers, Dates vary

What the books say

The books say that competitive intelligence is an effective, upright, and challenging activity which, at its best, bolsters a company's profitability, alerts it to opportunities, and protects it from external threats.

The books described in the previous chapter discuss a lot of aspects of the competitive intelligence process. Some themes recur, however, and we will divide our discussion into these categories:

1. **Identification** (of the information need).

2. **Collection** (of information).

3. **Analysis** (to turn information into knowledge).

4. **Reporting** (to get the knowledge to a decision-maker).

5. **Organization** (to make the four parts of the process work).

6. **Ethics** (to do things right and avoid difficulties later).

7. **Other issues** (some important matters that do not fit above).

The first four of these categories are phases or stages of the intelligence process. The last three cover issues which relate to the process. So, we begin at the beginning, with a question: What do you need to know?

1. **Identification** (of the information need):

Before you can answer a question, you have to have a clear question to answer. Otherwise you waste resources—and may not get where you need to go.

Some of the sources suggest an audit of competitive intelligence needs before establishing a CI function (Gilad, McGonagle/Vella). Certainly, on individual projects, the information goal must be clearly understood, or the probability of success shrinks markedly.

Porter's books make a persuasive and detailed case for the need for competitive information, and how it can be used.

Several sources provide guidance and in some cases checklists on what information to collect for company profiles, industry studies, etc.

In any case, the key to success in competitive intelligence is giving the decision maker the information he or she needs. Otherwise, the process is useless, the effort wasted. In order to meet the needs of the decision maker, the CI practitioner must do everything possible to understand clearly what those needs are.

This means asking the client all the questions necessary to understand the goal of the research. It may mean helping the client understand a goal that he or she may still be fuzzy about. It means that the CI researcher must, as much as possible, be an active part of planning for and applying the results of the research. A client may assume that the researcher understands what is wanted. A client may hope that the researcher understands what the client does not yet understand. A client may not want to share informa-

tion with the researcher for confidentiality reasons. All
three attitudes can cause problems down the road, however. They can result in too little information, too much
information, or just the right amount of information that
answers the wrong question.

2. **Collection** (of information):

Once you have the question pinned down, you need to
begin collecting information to help you answer it.

"Information is where you find it," is a good rule to follow,
the books suggest. Even though the most frequently used
sources may be database searches, interviews, or information from inside your own company, key facts can turn up
in the strangest places. It is good to keep an open mind,
and try new sources, as long as they are publicly accessible.

Fuld suggests a number of "creative" sources, such as
scanning classified ads, obtaining environmental impact
statements, and talking to shipping companies. The
Washington Researchers books have extensive lists of
"people sources" in federal and state governments, and the
researcher's own networking will lead to strange and
wonderful new friends.

Even though *information is where you find it*, the basic
sources of information are fairly straightforward:

Information from inside your company
Often, a great deal of information is available in your own
back yard. You have research reports and statistical
information already in the files, waiting to be pulled out,

pored over, compared and analyzed. And, more important, you have a ready-made information network, your
own colleagues. If you call Bill in R&D, he can tell you the
"state of the art" on a topic you are working on. He may
even have information on competitors that nobody ever
thought to ask him about before. Jennifer in marketing can
tell you how a marketer at your competitor might be
looking at his options, and she may even have first-hand
knowledge of competitor marketing strategies. And so on.
Use what you have.

Information from online databases
This book devotes entire chapters to both database sources
and people sources (next point). Briefly, databases provide
a gateway to enormous amounts of published information,
and they give you a powerful engine for motoring through
all that material and finding what you are looking for.
Basically, databases allow you to mobilize an army of
robot information finders to go scurrying around and find
what you want to know.

Information from people outside your company
When your internal sources falter and stall, when the
database trail disappears, knowledgeable people are where
you must turn. You locate them using names from published articles, source lists, recommendations from experts
you know, or just calling around. You ask them questions
and hope for good answers. One caveat: It is usually a
good idea not to call staff members of direct competitors.
Have an outside research firm do that. The outside firm
can identify itself, say it is working for a client (but not
necessarily identify the client), ask the questions, get the
answers (or not get the answers), and everything is open
and aboveboard.

After tapping all these sources, you may find you still do not have an answer. The CI literature seldom admits that this can happen, but it can. The company you need to know about is tiny or obscure; the question concerns business decisions that have not been made yet; the information involves true trade secrets or other confidential information that you should not be seeking. Then you or your client must formulate your best estimate based on what you can and do know.

The books have much more to say about the opposite situation, where you have so much information that you are drowning in it. That is where the next step, analysis, earns its money.

3. **Analysis** (to turn information into knowledge):

Raw information needs to be analyzed so that its value can be assessed and highlighted. Analysis and use of information is the core of the Porter books, and Mathey focuses on methodologies of analysis. However, the priorities of analysis vary with industry and project. The essential issue is to make the disparate information you have collected meaningful and useful.

The best analysis technique is the simplest: collect relevant information, absorb it, and consider its implications until they make sense. The goal is insight, not information. Information is dead unless it means something.

Number crunching to the contrary, analysis is more like making soup than assembling a machine. You put a lot of things into the pot, add heat, and wait for the mixture to become something else. Herbert Meyer, in his excellent book **Real World Intelligence,** puts it this way (p. 41):

> "Transforming raw information into finished
> intelligence is itself a step-by-step process.
> You study the raw material, argue and debate
> what the material means with your intelli-
> gence colleagues, check and recheck the facts,
> resolve the inevitable inconsistencies in the
> data, question your original assumptions,
> assure that as many acknowledged experts as
> possible have been consulted, develop some
> tentative theses, and then test these theses
> time and again until you are confident that
> the theses are valid."

That said, many paths lead to the big and little "eurekas"
of insight. Mathey (**Competitive Analysis**) discusses a
number of analysis approaches:

- Functional and chronological sorting (roadmaps):
  plotting the history of a company's development.

- Market share analysis: estimating key market shares
  for specific products.

- Organization charts: building approximate (not
  necessarily detailed) organization charts for competitors.

- Benchmarks: comparing specific performance points
  between own company and successful competitors.

- Product/service comparisons: looking at product
  overlap patterns and differing product mixes as
  guides to competitive position.

- Competitive stock market performance: plotting "value curves" to see how investors see company performance.

- Value chain analysis: compares the chain of production costs between two or more competitors.

- Strength and weakness analysis: assessing competitor strengths and weaknesses by function (e.g., engineering, manufacturing, marketing, finance, etc.)

- Vulnerability analysis: deciding whether a weakness actually represents a competitive vulnerability.

- Distinctive competence: identifying strengths which put a company clearly ahead of its competitors.

4. **Reporting** (to get the knowledge to a decision-maker):

Knowledge is worthless unless it gets to someone who can use it—and it has to arrive in usable form. When the sources discuss this issue, they usually emphasize that getting information to a decision-maker in a form perceived as useful is an essential success factor. This means at the very least a professional appearance, and perhaps extensive formatting, summarization, analysis, and text highlighting of report documents. Also, successful reporting requires a CI practitioner to build a strong professional relationship with the users of the intelligence product. If you do not have management's ear, you may be out on yours.

Gilad and Gilad devote a lengthy chapter (pp. 126-157) to issues of storage and dissemination of information.

Stanat's book, **The Intelligent Corporation**, focuses primarily on issues of information storage and retrieval. In sum, the storage and retrieval system must be "user friendly" and directly serve the goals of the CI program. It must build a wall against "information for information's sake," not become part of the problem.

With or without the support of a formalized information storage system, the reporting function is absolutely central to the success of the CI effort as a whole. Unheard, the CI message is meaningless. The books point out that the report format must be appropriate to the need and situation. Gilad and Gilad have specific guidance on report format options. They and others present the following options:

- Orally (in person, on the telephone, in a presentation to a group):

  This may be the method of choice for fast-moving situations, or CI information that is particularly sensitive. Some evaluative or interpretive comments on CI research may be communicated only orally. They may be too tentative to put in print, or they may represent judgments (as opposed to data) that do not belong in print for a variety of reasons.

  Presentations can be an efficient method for sharing data and then discussing its implications. In government and the military, the intelligence briefing is a time-honored tradition.

- In a one-page briefing sheet:

  A decision maker may want information distilled into its essence, and may not care so much about the background data that it rests on. This can be an excellent "selling tool" for the value of CI, especially if such bulletins are sent on a regular basis to people who can scan them quickly and feel they have learned something useful with minimal effort.

- In a typed or word-processed report to a single user:

  This may be brief or lengthy, but it will usually be focused on the requirements of one individual, with specific information that may not have relevance in a report for a broader audience. The information provided may have either tactical or strategic implications, or may simply inform the user about an area of potential interest.

- In a printed report to a number of users:

  Whether internal briefing papers or multiclient industry studies, these will be designed for easy understanding and breadth of purposes. For both single-user and multiuser studies, the presentation of a formal report should be as smooth and professional as possible. "The nicer it looks, the better it hooks" the reader, because the document communicates the care and effort that have gone into the project. The exception to this rule is when a handwritten or typewritten report would communicate the immediacy and time-urgency of a particular fact, event or insight.

- Through electronic mail:

  Increasingly popular where the organization's culture and equipment allow its use, electronic mail can provide excellent speed and accessibility in disseminating intelligence information. Such systems can control access on a need-to-know basis, as well as automatically routing new information to people who have registered their interest in specific subjects.

- Through an online computer system that users can access whenever they need it:

  The short word for this is "database." It means that the organization has spent the time and money to set up a central reservoir of information that anyone can tap on command, typically through a personal computer or terminal. Though a major investment, such a system can create a "community of information" in which users both obtain and provide information in a continuing dialogue. This dialogue serves to build and update the database, making it more useful to the information community as a whole.

5. **Organization** (to make the four parts of the process work):

The four steps above do not take place by magic. People's energies have to be harnessed to get the job done. One imperative is to keep the process relevant. Intelligence departments have foundered on the rocks of too much data, too many files, too few insights. The process has to be orderly, with ways that information can be reported by internal staff, collected from printed sources, analyzed and reported to users. But the organization should be lean and functional.

Two key success factors get emphasis in a number of sources. In addition to skilled researchers, CI operations need "coordinators" (individuals who oversee the intelligence process to make sure it works right) and "champions" (high achievers further up in the organizational hierarchy who fight to see that intelligence information is listened to, used—and supported).

6. **Ethics** (to do things right and follow the rules):

Too many people think competitive intelligence is spying. This misconception is not only wrong, it is dangerous, because it gets in the way of finding information effectively. An emphasis on ethical collection of information can set the record straight.

CI practitioners are usually on the right track if they keep in mind that they are dealing with public information. The books say public information is the following:

- Published information.
- Government documents (unless they are marked with a classification stamp such as "Secret" or "Confidential").
- Company information freely disclosed to an outside inquirer.

Public information is not:

- Trade secrets.

- Information that a company makes a diligent effort to protect.

- Information which has been obtained by covert or intrusive methods, such as wiretapping, electronic eavesdropping, or hiring a private plane to fly over a competitor's plant for photographs.

Even with this general guidance, grey areas can develop. It is best to discuss specific strategies with professionals (including legal advice). If still in doubt about an action, do not take it. Vella and McGonagle are particularly helpful in discussing these issues (**Outsmarting the Competition**, pp. 41-56).

Gordon, in **Beat the Competition!**, gives this guidance (p. 19):

> "If you are to develop superior strategies you will need quality competitive information. The temptation may be to acquire this information from whatever sources are available— even very 'marginal' ones. To draw the line between competitive intelligence and industrial espionage, refer ... to the definition of competitive intelligence:
>
> "'Competitive intelligence is the process of obtaining and analyzing publicly available data.'
>
> "It is the public availability of data that distinguishes the two. If anyone could legally

gather the data—if they only knew where to look, what to ask and how to ask it without misrepresenting themselves—then the activity can usually be considered legitimate."

David Parker, in "Legal Implications of Competitive Intelligence," a chapter in Sammon et al., **Business Competitor Intelligence**, summarizes the issue this way (p. 294):

"With the difficulties of making general statements on this subject firmly in mind, the following general rule is suggested: 'If you do not want to see what you are doing reported in the front-page headlines of your local newspaper, do not do it.' Needless to say, the analysis cannot stop at this point. What may be embarrassing may not necessarily be illegal. Nonetheless, this simple statement provides a surprisingly useful rule of thumb."

Kirk W. M. Tyson, in **Competitor Intelligence Manual & Guide**, points out (pp. 257-258):

"The process of gathering intelligence on your competitors should not be thought of as a war that must be won at all costs. Instead, it should be thought of as a game of strategy, and all games have rules.... The fact that senior managers love to play games of strategy suggests that intelligence activities always will be an integral part of the strategic management function in most companies. ... Nobody likes cheaters in any game. Being sportsmanlike means that you play by an agreed upon set of rules...."

All these writers agree that it is important to abide by the rules, to push for as much public information as you can find or obtain, but not to cross the line into unethical behavior.

7. Other issues:

Because competitive intelligence is a relatively young field, authors are still forming a consensus about what the key issues are.

Some authors like to describe what constitutes the practice and discipline of competitive intelligence and business research generally — activities involved and skills needed.

Writers who come out of government or military service sometimes discuss the differences between business intelligence and government/military intelligence. Military intelligence is not limited to public sources of information, for instance.

And being writers as well as CI experts, they usually cannot resist going off in directions that interest them and they hope will intrigue their readers.

All of which suggests: Read several books, not just one, to get a balanced view of what CI is now, and what it will likely become as it continues to evolve.

Finding the clues online

All generalizations are dangerous, but our experience has been that it's usually best to start a project with database searching. There are times when this should not be the case. Sometimes you know, or are reasonably sure, from past experience, that database searching is not going to be productive, but this is rare. The fewer the assumptions that are made at the beginning of a project the better, even for the experienced researcher.

Starting a project with database searching has a number of advantages.

- It will help define the project, if the subject of the search is something you are unfamiliar with.

- It will lead you to publications and people quoted or cited in the searches who can be sources of information themselves during later telephone work.

- It will suggest the wealth or lack of information available.

- It may accurately define and describe, if you are searching in a full-text database, the product or material you are researching.

If the subject is something the researcher is ignorant of, only full-text databases (where most or all of the article or document is provided) should be used at the outset. On at least one occasion we know of, researchers made the mistake of searching for an obscure chemical in databases containing nothing but abstracts (summaries) of articles from the periodical literature. There were two very different chemicals with one letter (an "n" rather than an "l") distinguishing between them. A number of abstracts led the researchers to focus on the "n" variant, and they proceeded to dive into the project, armed with this "infallible" (they had seen it in print with their own eyes, hadn't they?) information. Bad choice, as it turned out, They were into the second day of the project, searching databases and interviewing the wrong people, before realizing they really wanted the other variant. The result was arduous backtracking and re-interviewing, and a delayed but finally successful project.

Full-text database citations are often, particularly in technical or scientific fields, written by an authority or someone with considerable knowledge. But with an abstract of an article, as often as not the abstractor's expertise may lie largely in an ability to summarize and key-in data, and not lie at all in the subject at hand. Such expertise provides a fragile scaffolding on which to build a project. If you add your own ignorance of the subject to the abstractor's, the outcome can resemble the game of *Rumor* we played as children. One child tells another, that child tells yet another, and so on down the line, until the last child has to tell the group what he or she has heard. If you've ever played this game, you'll know the result was never a model of good communication. Communication theory has a model for this phenomenon, describing the stages rumors go through, but it may be sufficient to understand the dangers in building on any kind of verbal communication without verification or "second sourcing".

Even with these caveats, the capability to tap into computer-operated databases, retrieve information, and manipulate it using other computer functions, has several advantages over manual research (which often is still necessary anyway).

Some of these advantages are:

1. Access to an enormous variety of data nearly instan-
    taneously. (A variety and an amount of data beyond
    the dreams of a decade ago.)

2. The ability to scan this data quickly and to select
    criteria such as ranges of times or dates, etc...

3. After the data is retrieved, the ability to search
    through the selected block of data for key words and
    concepts.

4. The ability to arrange, edit and print this data elec-
    tronically.

Think of the electronic access to information as a tool, such
as a hammer. The hammer drives the nail of essential
information a lot faster than trying to push that nail in
with your hand or even hitting it with a rock.

In practice, the new database hammer drives a lot of
different nails. Online databases contribute to a competitive intelligence project by telling you:

1. Whether anything has been written on the question
    you need to answer.

2. Whether the articles, etc., answer the question.

3. If they don't answer the question, the database
    citations give you the name of the writer who might
    know the answer to the question, even if he did not
    write it in an article.

4. Database articles also give you the names of experts
    who have been consulted and quoted on the subject,
    so you can contact them, too.

5. Each of several database citations may provide a tidbit of information. When these tidbits are put together, they may reveal the answer, or at least suggest a likely estimate.

The interrelational capabilities of the databases are the key to this process. The computer's ability to ferret through information to find the nuggets of essential knowledge strengthens the researcher's ability to find actionable insights.

Leafing through books in a library seems infinitely laborious alongside this capability. However, a library's hard-copy resources (books and serials) still are a valuable and often essential part of the process. Databases skim the cream of knowledge, and mostly current knowledge. Before the middle 1980s, database coverage of published material gets sketchier and sketchier, and even now some useful research aids are not yet online.

Just as databases have their limitations when you go backward in time, they also often do not have the most current information, because of the lag time in indexing published materials. For current and future insights, you usually rely on the database results to tell you who will know the answers. Then you have to call these people on the telephone and ask questions directly. You will find a discussion of telephone interviewing techniques later in this book.

Choosing the databases to use
Let's take a more detailed look at the use of databases to develop competitive intelligence. Several types of databases exist (e.g., newspapers, magazines, trade publica-

tions, technical information, biographical profiles, company information, patents), and some are available on more than one gateway (or "vendor") service.

The sequence is usually to decide on the gateway and then to decide on the database.

You need to determine:

- What is your information need?
- What database format would best meet your need?
- What databases with that format cover the subject matter of your request?
- Do you need full-text, abstract or citation output?
- How much money should/can you spend?

Some examples of needs and solutions:

- You need a very recent report of quarterly financials for a public company. Choose the DOW JONES NEWS SERVICE, a gateway for financial information which includes full-text coverage of *The Wall Street Journal*. It provides timely access to these reports.

- You need to understand a subject you do not know much about. Use NEXIS, a full-text database organized so that you can browse through articles on a subject and retrieve only what you need.

- You need local newspaper coverage of a private company in Dallas. Access the *Dallas Morning News* on VU/TEXT to find local news articles on the company. You might also try BUSINESS DATELINE, a database on the DIALOG system which contains business-related articles from regional and local publications around the U. S.

- You want to find marketing information about a cosmetics product. Try PTS PROMT or PTS MARS, which contain articles from trade magazines/newspapers and general-interest business publications.

- You want to read the President's letter from the latest annual report for Procter & Gamble. Retrieve it on DISCLOSURE, a database which provides the contents of company filings with the U. S. Securities and Exchange Commission.

- You need information about methods of processing a food product. Try the FOOD SCIENCE AND TECHNOLOGY DATABASE.

- Want a quick snapshot briefing on a private company? Try DUN'S MARKET IDENTIFIERS or the COMPANY INTELLIGENCE database.

How do you get access to database material?

The first possibility is to do it yourself. You may already have this capability in the company library or in departments, or you may want to acquire the necessary computer, modem and software, and staff training to make use of database resources. However, the learning curve on database searching skills can be steep, and searchers should have enough work so that they search frequently.

Second, you can call your local public library. A significant percentage of public libraries are now offering database search services.

Third, you can use a research firm which will search the databases for you and send you the results.

What database options are available? Quite a number. But you do not need to access all of them to get what you need. Here are just some services and how they might be used:

A gateway service gives you access to a range of databases. Database suppliers band together under an umbrella organization that provides computer facilities and telephone access for large numbers of users. This centralizes the process of reaching individual databases. Otherwise, you'd have to remember a lot of phone numbers. DIALOG, for instance, currently has 383 databases, of which 50 to 70 are business-related, depending on how you count.

Some common gateways, in addition to DIALOG, are NEXIS, DOW JONES, DATA-STAR, NEWSNET, VU/TEXT, DATATIMES, ORBIT, COMPUSERVE, and BRS.

DIALOG offers information on public and private companies, both in the U. S. and internationally. DIALOG databases also provide information on products and markets. Material is available in either abstract or full-text (most or all of the article), depending on the database.

NEXIS also has broad coverage, but it is organized differently from DIALOG. It has a browsing format, where the searcher can page through full-text documents, reading everything or skipping around. It is especially good for an overall briefing on an industry, product or subject.

DOW JONES is the online source for the *Wall Street Journal* in full text, as well as other publications such as *Barron's* and the *Washington Post*. The Dow Jones News Wire gives quick access to breaking financial news.

DATA-STAR is a gateway to information about European companies. It has international D&B reports, and coverage from European newspapers, as well as some interesting specialty files.

ORBIT provides databases clustered in science, technology and patents, with some general business databases for spice. Chemistry, materials science, oil and natural gas, earth sciences, engineering, and patent literature are strengths of this gateway.

BRS is a general gateway similar to DIALOG but with more focus on medical and technical subjects. One strength is access to full-text medical journal articles. BRS also offers some unusual search protocols such as automatic searching of British and American variant spellings.

COMPUSERVE has a mix of services which reaches out beyond the business community to computer hobbyists and home users. The system provides shopping services and games along with business information. It also is interactive, with electronic mail service and online forums for discussion among people with a specific special interest. Of interest to business users are news reports, stock quotes, BUSINESS DATELINE with its articles from regional publications, and a "reference library" gateway to general databases. The "reference library" is menu-driven, meaning it leads you through the search process with on-screen instructions.

NEWSNET is a library of specialized newsletters organized by category. It covers, for example, advertising and marketing, biotechnology, chemicals, electronics, environment, health industry, manufacturing, real estate, telecommunications, and transportation. DIALOG also offers a newsletter database with similar coverage.

VU/TEXT is a full-text database of regional newspapers, for example, the *Arizona Republic*, the *Los Angeles Times*, the *Boston Globe*, the *Detroit Free Press*, and the *Chicago Tribune*. Most of the files go back to the middle 1980s, a few go back further, but recent additions to the system may only provide access back two or three years.

DATATIMES is another full-text newspaper database covering papers such as the *Louisville Courier-Journal*, the *Tulsa Tribune*, the *San Francisco Chronicle* and the *Dallas Morning News*. It also includes some international material, including extensive access to Canadian publications. Date coverage seldom goes back farther than 1985, and some files have two years or less.

DIALOG offers at least 50 databases of use to a business researcher. Some of the main ones:

> DUN'S MARKET IDENTIFIERS provides capsule profiles of some two million U.S. companies, both public and private.

> DISCLOSURE contains extracts from SEC filings for 11,000 public companies.

> DUN'S ELECTRONIC BUSINESS DIRECTORY is a listing of some 8.5 million U.S. businesses and professionals, useful for locating obscure companies.

HOPPENSTEDT DIRECTORY OF GERMAN COM-
PANIES is a bilingual directory of 35,000 German
companies.

ICC BRITISH COMPANY FINANCIAL
DATASHEETS and KOMPASS UK list British
companies.

CORPORATE AFFILIATIONS traces parent and
subsidiary ownership relationships. This database includes international corporate affiliations,
so that a corporation's domestic and foreign
subsidiaries can be tracked together.

INVESTEXT carries full-text investment analyst
reports on companies and industries. [NEXIS also
provides access to investment analyst reports.]

M&A FILINGS and IDD M&A TRANSACTIONS
contain information on mergers and acquisitions.
M&A FILINGS contains detailed abstracts of every
original and amended merger and acquisition
document released by the SEC since early 1985.
IDD M&A TRANSACTIONS covers completed
merger, acquisition or divestiture transactions
valued at $1 million or more.

BUSINESS DATELINE provides coverage of business news from a wide range of regional publications.

PTS PROMT gives extensive indexing and coverage of marketing activities by diverse industries.

PTS MARS covers marketing and advertising news, trends and developments.

TRADE & INDUSTRY INDEX provides citations and full-text in some cases for trade publication articles and corporate news releases.

PR NEWSWIRE is a continuously updated source for full-text company news releases.

MCGRAW HILL ONLINE provides full-text access to *Business Week* and other McGraw-Hill publications.

TRADEMARKSCAN follows trademark registrations, and several databases give access to patent registrations.

CLAIMS ™/U. S. PATENT ABSTRACTS describes patents listed in the general, chemical, electrical and mechanical sections of the Official Gazette of the U. S. Patent Office.

A good starting point is a general coverage business database such as PTS PROMT or TRADE AND INDUSTRY ASAP on DIALOG. An excellent non-business general coverage database on DIALOG is MAGAZINE ASAP. The last two mentioned are full-text databases.

For company information, DUN'S MARKET IDENTIFIERS or DUN'S ELECTRONIC BUSINESS DIRECTORY are useful, especially if the company is small and/or private. If it is a public company, a 10-K or 10-Q or a Proxy filing or some other filing may be available from DISCLOSURE.

COMPANY INTELLIGENCE provides a summary of company information, along with selected citations from recent articles. The producers of this database say they have contacted every listed company to verify data. If a company declines to provide information, this refusal is noted in the database record.

Regional newspaper databases can provide details on companies that do not have a national scope, and on events of a local or regional nature. We usually use BUSINESS DATELINE for a general sweep. If we know the locality, we go to DATATIMES or VU/TEXT, depending on which has relevant holdings. DATATIMES is a little easier to use, but both of them have unlocked difficult projects for us from time to time.

DISCLOSURE, and MOODY'S databases provide information about publicly-held corporations. STANDARD & POOR'S covers public and private companies.

The full-text browsing arrangement of the NEXIS system gives a good overview of a subject area, and helps the searcher identify the important issues, players and contact points (associations and individuals).

Searching online databases has a kind of grammar called "Boolean logic." If you enjoyed or were good at grammar in school, you should take to the search process. It has its own language patterns which follow fixed (and often non-intuitive) rules. The symbolic language saves time and space, both important when you go online. And for those with a bit of the writer in them, playing with the form of words and search statements can be a real pleasure. Of course, if you do not like symbols and grammar and fooling around with the way language is put together, it can drive you crazy. But database providers, interested in expanding their base of searchers, have tried to make it easier to search by providing various kinds of online help.

Searches can be as simple as scanning for a single word. More often, search statements combine words with Boolean connectors—"and," "or," "not"—and proximity instructions (one concept with a few words of another concept) to narrow the range of material retrieved.

For those who have not searched before, here is a brief example of how it works: Say you have heard about a new detergent product made by either Procter & Gamble or Unilever. You do not know the name of the product but you are sure it has been introduced in the current year. Just searching for "detergent" is likely to produce a flood of results, too much to deal with and most of it beside the point. You need to make the search statement much more specific. Two ways of doing this are with proximity and date ranges. Proximity allows you to ask for articles in which two key words appear close to each other (for example, "detergent" and "Procter"). Date ranges let you specify the dates you want to scan ("published in 1991" or "between 3/1/91 and 9/30/91"). You might also want to eliminate some words to narrow your results ("detergent not soap"). A working search statement might go something like this: detergent within 10 words of Procter published in 1991 not mentioning soap. That should give you a very focused group of results, hopefully containing a description of the product you are hunting.

This search process lets you go through massive amounts
of published information with speed and precision. The
computer does most of the scanning work for you, eliminating material you are not interested in so that you can
page through only those materials that might hold the
information you are looking for. It's like having thousands
of journalists and researchers on your staff assembling
information for you.

And that information is not just U. S. anymore. Information resources on European companies are becoming more
available, and demand for them is being pushed both by
the economic "unification" of Europe (EC 1992) and the
opening of Eastern European economies to Western enterprise. And the most efficient source for European information is often a database. Corporate profile information,
financial data, and marketing activities can be tracked this
way. Chapter Nine discusses sources of online information
about European markets and companies.

Whether the information you need is domestic or international, the flow of the project is similar. It generally goes
this way:

Design the search strategy
We try to keep strategies as simple as possible, while at the
same time using the available short cuts. For the sake of
continuity, let's assume we are working under the DIALOG
command format; the principles often apply to other
database formats as well.

Subject searches can be approached either through free-
text searching (looking for specific words or phrases in the
text of an article) or codes for particular products or activities. It is good to go beyond the terms your client has

given you to find likely synonyms. Say you want to find
out what kind of consumer complaints can be expected
after the launch of a new skin care product. The exact
request from the client is: "Find any information about
public dissatisfaction with hand creams."

A free-text search strategy for this request might look
something like:

s ((skin or hand)(2w)(cream or lotion)) (10w)(dissatisfaction or reject? or critic? or complain? or fail?)

In ordinary language, this strategy translates as: create a
set number for *skin* or *hand* when it is two words or less
away from *cream* or *lotion* and then look for this combination within 10 words of *dissatisfaction* or *reject* (and longer
words with this beginning, like *rejected* or *rejection* or
rejecting) or *critic* (and longer words like *critics, critical,
criticism,* etc.) or...

Product codes are one way to reach for comprehensive
coverage, although it is important to realize that they are
as dependent on the indexer's decision as your free-text
search is dependent on your choice of synonyms. The
codes are multidigit numbers which stand for types of
products. Predicasts databases such as PROMT and MARS
have excellent product-code indexing, built on but not
identical to the Standard Industrial Classification (SIC)
system. An example of a Predicasts code is 33315 for
copper alloys.

Array searching can be useful, especially when helping a
client locate companies in a mergers and acquisitions
search. Arrays are simply lists of similar entities. Array
searching allows you to group companies by SIC code or

sales or location or other factors, or several factors at once.
So you can build a list of tire companies in Akron, Ohio,
with sales in excess of $100 million. The principle is the
same, really, as when you create a set of article abstracts
about toothpaste published since January 1, 1988.

To build an array, you might use a strategy like this on
DUN'S MARKET IDENTIFIERS:

   s sa=50M:500M and sf=headquarters and zp=60611

This search yields 40 companies with $50 million to $500
million in sales, headquartered in downtown Chicago.
Addition of a pc= or sc= limiter would narrow the search
further to companies with a particular product or service.

Global searching accesses several databases during the
same search and can be a useful and cost-effective way to
achieve several goals:

• Identifying which databases would be most useful
  for a particular inquiry

• Getting a quick overview of the topic from several
  sources.

• Seeing how much abstracted material, or full-text
  material, is out there on the topic.

• Seeing if anything is out there at all.

The results of this reconnaissance can really make you
appreciate enhancements like multi-file searching options.
Database gateways like DIALOG and DATA-STAR are made
up of many discrete files that you search one at a time.
This usually is fine, because you are focusing on a particular subject area. But sometimes you want to know what is

available on a particular topic across several different data files. DATA-STAR's "CROS" and DIALOG's "ONESEARCH," among others, allow you to scan many files in one search, instead of plodding along file to file in just a straight line. In contrast, a strength of the NEXIS system is that it is essentially one big file with everything in together, so you search across many subject areas in a normal search.

And SDI's (selective dissemination of information) can make systematic tracking of a company or an issue easier. An SDI is a search strategy that runs periodically, for instance, every month. The idea is to keep track of developments in a systematic way, so you are alerted promptly to important events and nothing gets missed. SDI's supply a predictable flow of information and are a good hedge against missing something important. Some online services are arranged so that SDI's can be set up online. After that, they will run automatically at a set interval, typically each time the database is updated. Another option is to save each SDI search strategy on your communications software, so you can run it on command.

Review and edit your results

This is an important part of the process. We have found that our clients care deeply about how information is presented to them. They want it relevant, they want it categorized, and they want it in a clean, attractive format that is easy to read. Sometimes, but not always, they want some analysis.

We try to make sure that every database "hit" (or citation) is either directly relevant to the client's request, or if it is only tangentially relevant, that the relevance is explained in a note above the citation. This can be tricky, because one person's relevance is another person's waste of time. But it

is almost always a mistake to pour out uncategorized data
rather than trying to make some sense of it. Organizing
information is at the heart of competitive intelligence. The
potential for making connections between disparate pieces
of information may be enhanced simply by shaping and
rearranging the pieces.

Adding value to information can be done in several de-
grees. For instance, you can divide it into three increasing
levels of working with database results:

1. **As a minimum**, strip the citations of "housekeep-
    ing" information, anything that will not be
    helpful to the user of the information. This could
    mean codes that users will not understand,
    descriptor lists that they do not need, categories
    that have no relevance to their questions.

2. **The next level**: Group database citations accord-
    ing to subject. A search describing a competitor
    might be divided into basic description (address,
    etc.) subsidiaries, management, products, market-
    ing strategy, financials, operations, acquisitions/
    divestitures, or whatever else the user needs to
    know.

3. **The third level**: Analyze the information and
    derive conclusions not explicitly stated in the
    search results.

Seemingly unrelated items of published information, when
nudged up side-by-side, can reveal some interesting
insights. The following example shows how this might be
done using database sources alone:

As a hypothetical example, say you need to know
the sales of X Company, Inc., a small privately
held supplier of lard in Ohio. Your database
searches turn up several interesting items. A
newspaper article about a food poisoning inci-
dent at an elementary school in Clyde, Ohio,
mentions that X Company has recalled 5,000
cases of lard, its entire production for the week of
November 8. A report on a new method of
packaging states that wholesale lard is always
packaged in 20-pound lots. And another article
says that the wholesale price of lard averages 25
cents a pound. A little arithmetic gives you a
credible estimate of X's annual sales: 5,000 cases
times 52 weeks gives 260,000 cases; 260,000 cases
times 20 pounds per case gives 5,200,000 pounds;
5.2 million pounds times 25 cents gives $1.3
million estimated sales of lard for X Company.

Produce some form of output to give to the client
Different formats are required to suit different situations.

Sometimes a phone call to report the results is enough.
Most often, a printout of search results (always edited
either lightly or heavily) is required. And some projects
demand a laser-printed bound analysis with charts and
other illustrations.

The output is at least as important as the search:

- It has to arrive on time, when it is needed.
- It has to be easy to read, to understand, and to use.

- It has to reach someone who can use it.
- It has to convey a standard of professionalism, so it will be credible.

A telephone call is the fastest and simplest, of course. But it can convey only simple, brief information. Anything complex usually needs to be delivered in written form.

Sometimes a printout of database results is all that is necessary. But it usually needs to be edited to eliminate the housekeeping material such as search strategies, codes, and introductory announcements. And often the database hits should be grouped by topic instead of provided in random order or database-by-database.

And when any analysis is required, a smooth written report is, too.

After all this detail on databases, you may be experiencing MEGO ("my eyes glaze over"). So this may be a good time to point out that databases are not always the best solution to research problems. It may be more effective to head for an in-house, university or public library to find the answers. Hard-copy (books and periodicals) is still an important source of information, the deep places under the surface of the database coverage.

Some information clearly is NOT available online. It may have been published before databases existed to index it, or perhaps no commercial database covers that particular kind of information. Or you may choose to consult a directory or other resource at a library rather than electronically.

Whether you find your information on a database or from some other source, you will be very fortunate to find all the answers in a single article. Often a fact from one article needs to be put together with facts from other articles. Then you can see correlations and draw inferences. Databases can save you a lot of time and team you up with other smart people working to understand how one little piece of the universe is put together. Imagine sending out a message and having the entire staff of *The New York Times* as well as the faculty of Columbia University help you solve a problem. That is what databases can do for you.

Directory of online database gateway services ("vendors") cited in this chapter

BRS™

    BRS Information Technologies
    8000 Westpark Drive
    McLean, VA 22102-9980
    (800) 955-0906

COMPUSERVE®

    Compuserve
    P. O. Box 20212
    Columbus, OH 43220
    (614) 457-8650
    (800) 848-8990

DATA-STAR

    RadioSuisse
    D-S Marketing, Inc.
    485 Devon Park Drive
    Wayne, PA 19087
    (215) 687-6777
    (800) 221-7754

DATATIMES®
   Datatimes
   14000 Quail Springs Parkway, Suite 450
   Oklahoma City, OK 73134
   (405) 751-6400

DIALOG^{SM}
   DIALOG Information Services Inc.
   3460 Hillview Avenue
   Palo Alto, CA 94304
   (415) 858-3785
   (800) 334-2564

DOW JONES NEWS RETRIEVAL®
   Dow Jones & Company, Inc.
   P.O. Box 300
   Princeton, NJ 08543-0300
   (609) 452-1511

NEWSNET®
   NewsNet Inc.
   945 Haverford Road
   Bryn Mawr, PA 19010
   (215) 527-8030
   (800) 345-1301

NEXIS®
   Mead Data Central
   9443 Springboro Pike
   P.O. Box 933
   Dayton, OH 45401
   (513) 859-1608
   (800) 543-6862

ORBIT®
>   ORBIT Search Service
>   8000 Westpark Drive
>   McLean, VA 22102-9980
>   (800) 955-0906

VU/TEXT®
>   Vu/Text Information Services, Inc.
>   325 Chestnut Street
>   1300 Mall Building
>   Philadelphia, PA 19106
>   (215) 574-4400
>   (800) 258-8080

Going online for
Japanese information

Along with the growth of databases in the U. S., but lagging it somewhat, has been the growth in databases containing information about Japan. This new availability of Japanese information has come none too soon.

Following WW II, Japan began its economic expansion with a global strategy of price, then followed with one of quality, and now pursues a technological edge, an edge partially attainable within America's open knowledge community. The strong yen has made Japan an even more capable competitor, and at the same time, ever-increasing competition from Taiwan, South Korea and other newly industrialized economies is forcing Japan to branch out into new industries now dominated by the U.S. as aerospace, supercomputers, telecommunications, financial services, and biotechnology. The Japanese will soon hit the U.S. with a whole new round of high-technology products, according to one source.[15]

The series of competitive pushes from Japan into the U.S. in the past decades should leave little doubt that America will continue to lose its competitive position within the global marketplace in the years to come.

It is common knowledge in the information industry that for years, JETRO (a research arm of the Ministry of International Trade & Industry or MITI), and JICST (a quasi-governmental organization funded by Japan's Science & Technology Agency) have been systematically gathering foreign technical and business information for Japanese businesses.[16]

A survey published by MITI in 1989 reported a total of 1,964 commercial databases available in Japan, of which 1,436 were of foreign origin, compared to 528 databases that were originally produced in Japan. This represents dramatic growth in the number of databases accessible: Japan had access to only 456 databases in 1982. This represents a growth of some 300 databases per year!

The same MITI survey reported that the number of foreign databases accessible in Japan includes those available through familiar major gateways such as DIALOG, ORBIT, and so on.

Of the $300 million spent in Japan on database services in 1988, some 70% was spent on Japanese databases, and the remainder on "foreign" databases. Presumably, since American databases dominate the global electronic marketplace today, Japan is spending a great deal of the remaining $100 million (30%) on U.S. databases.

But U.S. researchers can also look across the Pacific to Japan via database. Here is a listing of English language databases available in the U.S. and covering Japan, and some more detailed profiles of Japanese databases:

(Note: Some of the following material is from a U.S. Department of Commerce NTIS publication titled: **Directory of Japanese Databases PB-90-163080**. In a telephone conversation with Janet Geffner, the series editor with National Technical Information Service, she reminded us of the valuable Japanese technical and scientific "grey-literature" that NTIS holds, and thus of the access Americans and others have to Japanese corporate and technical information, should they choose to use it.)

English–Language Japanese Databases		
Database	**Type**	**Availability**
COMLINE	Japan's technology and industry	GEnie and DIALOG/PTS[17]
DRI Japanese Forecast	Macroeconomics	Data Resources
HIASK/Asahi Shimbun	Full text from daily newspaper	HINET/ NEXIS[18]
IBJ DATA	Earnings reports 100 companies	GEnie
Japan Computer Industry Scan	R&D/Industry/ Marketing	NewsNet (EC-39)
Japan Economic Daily	Full text newswire/ high-tech	Dow Jones
Japan Economic Journal	Daily econ, newspaper	Nexis (File JEJ)
Japan Economic Newswire	News service full text	Dialog (File 612)
Japan Free Press	Abstracts, various media	NewsNet (Code IT 6)
Japan High Tech Review	Electronics/ telecommunications/ computers	NewsNet (Code EC 28)

Database	Type	Availability
Japan Semiconductor Scan	Trends/U.S. and Japan	NewsNet (Code EC)
Japan Weekly Monitor	Tokyo stock exchange	NewsNet (Code IT2)
Japan Aviation News: Wing	Industry/scientific traffic	NewsNet (Code AE)
Japanese Industry Competitive Intelligence Tracking Service	Japanese industry	SIS, Inc.[19]
JAPIO (Japan Patent Information Service)	Abstracts and drawings	Pergammon/ Orbit
JED/Japan Economic Daily	Economics/financial business/politics	Kyodo News International[20]
JETRO-ACE	Trends overseas economy/trade	Heiwa Information
JIJI Stock Price Data Bank	Stocks in Tokyo, Osaka, New York	GEnie

Database	Type	Availability
JICST	Science and technology	National Technology Information Service
KENS/Kyodo English News Service	General/economy political/business	
New Era: Japan	Telecommunications	NewsNet (Code TE 70)
NIKKEI Construction	Monthly time-series construction	Nikkei Telecom/ Needs-Net
NIKKEI Energy	Monthly time-series energy	Nikkei Telecom/ Needs-Net
NIKKEI Sangyo Shimbun Articles	Full text newspaper	Nikkei Telecom/ Needs-Net
NIKKEI Telecom Japan News Retrieval	Stocks/bonds/ economy	
NKS Article Information D.B.	Abstracts/ economics journals	Nikkei Telecom/ Needs-Net
NRI/E Japan Economic and Business	Time-series data/ economy/industry/ product forecasts	GEnie

Selected Japanese Databases in Depth
English and Japanese Language

JAPIO
Subject coverage: Science and technology
Language: English
Database Description:

This English language database produced by the Japan Patent Information Organization (JAPIO), contains more than two million Japanese patent application records since 1976. Records consist of bibliographic information, an abstract, International Patent Classification Codes and Japanese Patent Classification Codes.

This is the English version of a subset of the Japanese-language Patolis/Patent and Utility Models databases operating in Japan. The JAPIO file excludes records of patent applications that are thought to be of interest only to the Japanese, as well as records of utility models.

Producer: Japan Patent Information Organization
Telephone: 011-81-3-503-3900

Access: Online access is through the Orbit Search Service of Maxwell Online, Inc.
Telephone: (800) 421-7229 or (703) 442-0900

JICST Science, Technology and Medical Document File/ JICST-E
Subject coverage: Science and technology
Language: English
Database Description:

Contains article records from more than 4,000 periodical titles, technical reports, government documents and conference papers published in Japan since 1985, in the fields of science, technology and medicine. The database contained some 900,000 records as of 1990. Approximately 15-30% of the records in the file currently have English abstracts.

Producer: Japan Information Center of Science & Technology/Tokyo, Japan
Telephone: 011-81-3-581-6411 (ext. 445) or: Japan Information Center of Science & Technology/Washington, DC/
Telephone: (202) 872-6372

Access: NTIS
Telephone: (703) 487-4822 or: STN International c/o Chemical Abstracts Service
Telephone: (800) 848-6533, or (614) 447-3600 or:
Mitsubishi International Corp. New York, NY
Telephone: (212) 605-1890

Intellectual Property Law Cases (Chiteki Shoyuken Hanrei Detabesu)
Subject coverage: Science and technology
Language: Japanese
Database Description:

This full text database covers roughly 7,500 cases dating back to the year 1900, in the field of intellectual property laws, including patents, designs, utility models, trademark, copyright, and antitrust cases. Only select fields are available online, however, and the copies of the original cases are made available offline. New cases are added to the file 6 months after judgment.

Producer: Kinki University/Osaka, Japan
Telephone: 011-81-723-67-0111

Access: Online access through HINET via Tymnet. Tokyo, Japan
Telephone: 011-81-3-349-7791

Chinese Information (Chugoku Joho)
Subject coverage: Business, economics, finance, science & technology.
Language: Japanese
Database Description:

The database covers, in Japanese, articles published in 60 major Chinese newspapers. About 70 articles are added to the file each week, covering 13 industrial fields, including automotive, electronic, fashion and textiles, construction, energy and oil, plant projects, travel and leisure, and law and government policy.

Producer: Databank Company, Ltd., Tokyo, Japan
Telephone: 011-81-3-760-7651

Access: Online access through HINET via Tymnet. Tokyo, Japan
Telephone: 011-81-3-349-7791

Food Industries Data File/ JAFIC
Subject coverage: Food science and technology
Language: Japanese
Database Description:

This Japanese-language bibliographic database provides references from more than 160 periodical titles and 60 technical reports in areas related to the food industry, including the processing and packaging of food, nutritional and toxicology information, government guidelines and regulations, as well as marketing and management information. It contained some 26,000 records as of 1990.

Producer: Japan Food Industry Center/Tokyo, Japan
Telephone: 011-81-3-591-7451

Access: NTIS/Springfield, VA
Telephone: (703) 487-4822

Market Search (Maaketto Sachi)
Subject coverage: Business, economics and finance.
Language: Japanese
Database Description:

This database provides coverage of marketing information published in a variety of Japanese news media, including newspapers, magazines, monthly reports of financial institutions, ad-hoc market survey reports from associations and research consulting firms, as well as data published by the Japanese government, dating back to August, 1984. Some 160,000 records were in the file as of 1990. File is updated monthly.

Producer: JMA Research Institute/Tokyo, Japan
Telephone: 011-81-3-434-1721

Access: Online access through HINET via Tymnet. Tokyo, Japan
Telephone: 011-81-3-349-7791

NIKKEI Telecom II—Japan Financial News & Data
Subject coverage: General
Language: English and numerical
Database Description:

Nikkei Telecom II is a comprehensive and integrated English-language information service, offering full-text news articles, and economic and business information from Japan. It provides database, electronic mail, bulletin board services, as well as Japanese PC network access, graph and table generation, and automatic data retrieval scheduling capabilities. The service offers major articles translated from the morning edition of the *Nihon Keizai Shimbun* (Nikkei—Japan's top business newspaper), as well as major articles from the *Japan Times* (Japan's leading English-language daily), offering a comprehensive coverage of politics, society, economics and business before the newspapers are delivered. Also covers more than 50 weekly and monthly newsletters, business reports on banks and trading firms, and technical reports of high-tech firms.

Producer: Nihon Keizai Shimbun America, Inc./New York, NY
Telephone: (215) 512-3600

Access: As above.

JETRO ACE
Subject coverage: Business, economics and finance.
Language: Japanese and numerical
Database Description:

JETRO ACE reports on regional economies and provides trade and investment information on 101 countries collected by JETRO's overseas offices. The file is updated weekly.

Producer: Japan External Trade Organization (JETRO)/Tokyo, Japan
Telephone: 011-81-3-587-2836

Access: Online access through HINET via Tymnet. Tokyo, Japan
Telephone: 011-81-3-349-7791

EL-NET
Subject coverage: General topics
Language: Japanese
Database Description:

Provides full-text articles in Japanese from 33 newspapers and 253 periodicals published in Japan. The articles are fully indexed and stored as digitized images in their optical disk storage. Users can perform keyword searches to obtain original article copies via fax or mail. EL-NET also offers SDI service. The database's coverage breaks down as follows: industry 47.8%, economy 25.5%, politics 11.6%, science 3.2%, society 8.7%, and culture 3.2%. EL-NET is adding some 500,00 to 600,00 article records annually.

Producer: Electronic Library, Inc./Tokyo, Japan
Telephone: 011-81-3-779-1212

Access: Contact Electronic Library, listed above. Direct online access via Venus-P, to EL-NET's host computer in Japan. Plans to make their service directly from U.S. in the future.

[15] **Directory of Japanese Databases:** 1990, U.S. Department of
      Commerce, NTIS, 1990, p. 3.

[16] **Directory of Japanese Databases:** 1990, U.S. Department of
      Commerce, NTIS, 1990, p. 4.

[17] Most of the COMLINE reports are available through PTS
      30 days after the original COMLINE reports are issued.

[18] Selected articles are available from this newspaper database
      through NEXIS with a two-day delay.

[19] Strategic Intelligence Systems, Inc. Available online and on
      CD-ROM. New York, NY 1001, (212) 725-1550

[20] Kyodo News International, New York, NY, (212) 586-0152.

[21] Heiwa Information Center Company, Ltd. One source
      indicated JETRO-ACE is available here through a line from
      Japan to Tymnet. Also available on CD-ROM.

[22] National Technical Information Service, Springfield, VA,
      (703) 487-4822.

Going online for
European information

Information resources on European business and European companies are proliferating, as the demand for them is being driven by the economic "unification" of Europe and the opening of Eastern European economies to Western enterprise.

Given the pressing speed of events in Europe, the most viable sources for information are a database or a telephone. Corporate profile information, financial data, credit reports, product information, marketing activities and much else besides can be tracked online. But which database will best do the job?

Commercial database gateways access a growing wealth of European material, and the European Community itself maintains databases available to U. S. users through TYMNET. DIALOG, NEXIS, DATA-STAR, DATATIMES and VU/TEXT are five commercial database services which have European information of various types and formats. Each could be the service of choice, depending on your need. Similar resources may be found on many of them. Exclusive access to a resource is the exception.

DIALOG
DIALOG provides access to some 400 separate databases. Thirteen of these are focused solely on international companies, including EUROPEAN DUN'S MARKET IDENTIFIERS, HOPPENSTEDT DIRECTORY OF GERMAN COMPANIES, ICC BRITISH COMPANY DIRECTORY, and KOMPASS EUROPE. Other DIALOG databases contain international material of one kind or another. PTS PROMT has both U.S. and international marketing information, and a code for

the European Community helps focus your search strategy. INFOMAT INTERNATIONAL BUSINESS has English
abstracts from periodicals in 10 languages. International
company databases can be searched all at once with an
umbrella code (ONESEARCH INTLCO category). And, in
December of 1990 DIALOG opened access to a comprehensive source of U.S. import-export data—the *Journal of
Commerce* PIERS database.

LEXIS-NEXIS
Mead Data Central (LEXIS and NEXIS) offers EUROPE, its
new library focused specifically on Europe and EC, and
designed with the international business researcher in
mind. Briefly, the library includes a news section, company
information from the EXTEL database, four categories of
analytical material, and full text or abstracts of EC legislation and debates. The news section covers some 30 news
sources. The legislative section includes the full text of the
CELEX database (the contents of the Official Journal of the
European Communities documenting European Community legislation).

NEXIS' general library of publications cuts a wide swath
and also includes international material; it can be searched
for current material or anything back to the earliest articles
in the database.

DATA-STAR
DATA-STAR is a Europe-based system organized much like
DIALOG; it provides access to French and German newspapers, international Dun & Bradstreet reports, and European technical information. Some DATA-STAR material is
in French and German as well as English.

DATA-STAR is seeing a new crossover usage among its U.S. customers. Users who once accessed only trade statistics (TRADSTAT) are now crossing over to use the interactive databases for focused searches on marketing opportunities. This suggests a broader, more sophisticated use of information, a greater demand for marketing inferences and insights, going beyond just the hard numbers. DATA-STAR also plans to expand its resources to include more material on Eastern Europe and Asia.

Two databases known primarily for their coverage of regional U.S. newspapers also function as gateways to international material:

DATATIMES
DATATIMES provides access to regional newspapers and magazines. Its international strength is in Canadian materials; but it also connects to European Community and EC 1992 information, including the CELEX database.

VU/TEXT
VU/TEXT also provides access to the CELEX database documenting EC legislation, as well as other international materials in the London Financial Times PROFILE resources. You need a separate password in VU/TEXT to use this gateway service.

European Community Access
The European Community has three groups of databases accessible from the U.S.: Eurobases (CELEX, SCAD, and Info-92); ECHO; and statistical databases. Statistical databases are only accessible through Wharton Econometrics.

Some of this EC material is in English; but other portions
are in various European languages. The CELEX database,
with information on EC legislation, is available directly
from the EC, but must be searched using Mistral v, a query
language not noted for its user friendliness. CELEX is also
available to U.S. users through NEXIS, VU/TEXT and
DATATIMES.

In addition to Eurobases, there are two other groups of EC
databases:

ECHO (European Community Host Organization) has
some databases that are free of charge. ECHO databases
include: DIANEGUIDE, a directory of European databases;
ARCOME, a list of organizations doing research in the
communications field; BIOREP, with biotechnology research projects being done in EC member states; EURO-
DIACAUTOM, useful for current translations of technical
terms in any EC languages but Greek; JUSLETTER, summa-
rizing initiatives taken in community law (intended for
lawyers); SESAME, online source for energy projects supported by the EC; and TED, from the "S" supplement of the
Official Journal containing public calls for tender from
some 80 countries (documents are available the morning of
publication).

Three EC statistical databases are available only through
Wharton Econometrics—CRONOS, COMEXT and REGIO.
CRONOS has time series on everything from commodities
prices to export figures, and is the comprehensive database
for such statistics. Time series in this database go back to
the sixties. COMEXT covers external trade statistics. REGIO
has economic and social statistics.

For a comprehensive article on EC databases by an EC authority, see Colin Hensley's article in *Database*, December, 1989, titled "European Community Databases."

Interviewing

People are important in finding business information, whether from your own personal network of knowledgeable sources outside the company's staff, or from others you can identify and contact. People know a lot more than books do about current business situations. Even though some of this information is proprietary, much of it would be freely provided if someone would ask for it. Database searches and hard-copy research will yield the names and affiliations of experts in your topic. Then it is time to go to the telephone and start talking to the people mentioned in those database citations, asking them the questions that the research suggests but does not answer.

Often a good place to start is right inside your own company. Staff members know a lot of competitive information they may never have been asked to share.

You may need to use your network of contacts within your company, for instance. The sales force, which operates on the front lines, usually has access to many interesting facts about the competitive situation. The key is to obtain this information efficiently. One way is through informal contacts with individual salesmen, either by telephone or through electronic mail. It is a good idea to provide incentives to sales people who contribute, such as trading information or providing regular bulletins that will help them do their jobs. An elaborate formal reporting system often becomes unwieldy and falls into disuse.

Beyond the sales force, it is important to find alert and curious individuals throughout the organization who can be queried on a regular basis. Scientists in R&D often know what their counterparts are working on, or they can advise on the likely truth or reliability of doubtful information. The same is true of plant managers, financial officers and other staff experts who know how your business works—and often a good deal about competitors as well.

To build an effective internal intelligence system, however, two things are required:

- **a coordinator** who can make the contacts, put the pieces together and draw conclusions, and

- **a champion**, a fast-rising or senior manager in the organization who can make sure you get the support you need to succeed.

But you may still need to ask someone outside the "friendly confines" of your own company. We try to keep in mind that no matter how small a company or a product is, it is important to someone. Once you've figured out who cares about the product or company, you can start making phone calls. In one instance the small company we were interested in happened to be located in a small town, so identifying interested parties was simple enough to do. This importance factor is always significant. Others to whom a product or company might be important, beyond the city in which the plant is located, would be trade publications, the product distributor, industry watchers in Washington, competitors, regulatory or licensing agencies, agencies who issue building permits, and so on.

If someone has publicly commented on a company we are interested in, that source is often more willing to respond to phone calls about their remarks. Quite often they are much more candid on the telephone than they were in the article.

Some knowledgeable individuals to contact:

- **Company officers**
- **Customers**
- **Suppliers**
- **Government officials**
- **Journalists**
- **Competitor managers**
- **Trade association managers**
- **Academic experts**

The first thing to remember in telephone information gathering is that competitive intelligence is about *public* behavior and the public information it generates. Markets are public forums, and companies that participate in markets are involved in a public activity. When you make telephone calls to a company, you do not seek proprietary information about that company, information that companies can reasonably keep secret, such as product formulas or manufacturing processes.

Not everyone is comfortable with telephone research, to say the least. It takes a little bit extra to pick up the telephone and ask a stranger a bunch of possibly nosey questions. But telephone interviewing is a mandatory part of many CI projects.

Several reasons encourage people to talk to you, and in a properly conducted telephone interview, both sides can gain. For one thing, knowledgeable people often find it helpful to talk through a question, especially when a skillful questioner is doing the prompting. Second, they may enjoy sharing their expert knowledge with you.

Third, they may learn useful things from the kinds of questions you ask (although it is usually not proper to disclose your client's name without permission to do so). Fourth, you may be able to trade information with them, something you learned from a database search for example, for something they know. Fifth, some sources want to enhance their professional reputation by providing your client with information, or they may have some other self-interest in helping you understand a subject or situation.

Good telephone interviewing takes more than the gumption to make some calls. It also takes planning. Usually telephone information gathering is very focused, very targeted. You need to decide what you want to know. You may want to list your information objectives in an order of priority, or jot down a few important questions, or even create a formal script where everything is spelled out in detail (important for controlled survey work). Usually a telephone interview is a combination of targets and serendipity. You make sure to get what you need, if you can, and after that maybe allow the conversation to wander a bit, in case you hear a new insight or piece of information you did not know to ask for.

Interviewing is an art. The process of asking the right questions and getting the right answers requires practice and finesse. Knowing more about the process is a good place to begin, however:

1.   Plan the interviews.

2.   Ask easy questions first, then harder ones.

3.   Save conversation stoppers for the end.

4.   Do not ask questions that you know your source must not answer.

5. Ask questions several different ways. If you are blocked one way, ask in another.

6. Be polite but be persistent.

7. Ask for references to other individuals or published sources. ("Is there someone else who ..."; "Is there an article that might be useful ..."; "Do you have that person's phone number ..."; "...the citation of the article?")

8. Contact everyone you can think of until you get enough clues to at least estimate an answer.

Should you interview in person or on the telephone?

In-person interviewing:
1. is much more time-consuming and costly.

2. allows for a deeper discussion.

3. allows the interviewer to build better rapport with the subject.

4. may involve helpful demonstrations or plant tours.

Telephone interviewing:
1. is more efficient if you are looking for a specific answer to a specific question.

2. requires a keen ear, single-focus concentration, and agile questioning.

Both types can be standardized through using a preprinted questionnaire for each interview.

Sometimes the universe of contacts is small and well-defined, with only a few significant contacts within an industry, all of them known to you. More often, however, you do not know who can be most helpful to you. In fact, you often do not know the existence of the sources who eventually will unlock the project for you. You must simply begin to call the people you know, ask the questions, and then ask for referrals to people who may know the specific facts you need. This process may involve tens or even hundreds of phone calls, but the payoff at the end of the project is considerable.

If sources become reluctant in either face-to-face meetings or telephone interviews, you can use several techniques to reassure them. Tell them you are not seeking anything secret or proprietary, but simply information that can be publicly disclosed. If the person is still uncomfortable, you might say something like "You seem bothered by this line of questioning" and shift to another subject. You might try later to return to those problem questions by using different terms or approaches.

Always be courteous, and give your source the impression (certainly a correct one!) that you appreciate and value what he or she is telling you. Be upbeat and obviously interested. If the source says something you do not understand, ask for more explanation. Humility is an excellent interviewing technique, and it usually is sincere, because you are looking for something you do not know. That said, some knowledge of the industry or subject is helpful, because it tells the source that you have done your homework and are likely to understand sophisticated comments about the subject.

Persist firmly but gently until you get your answers or are totally and irrevocably blocked. Sometimes you need to ask that one last question, that one additional question that you may hesitate to ask, but that might draw out a deeper and sometimes all-important answer.

Interviewing is often essential to a project because the information you seek has never been collected and published anywhere. Even though it may be public in nature and freely available to anyone who asks, you have to go and ask for it. And you may have to ask a bunch of people and then put the facts together to reach a conclusion that none of those people has figured out yet. This process can make you the sole possessor of an answer no one else in the whole world knows, which is pretty exciting stuff. The answers are right there for the asking—and asking, and asking, and asking.

One caveat: It usually is not a good idea to call or contact competitors directly for an interview. Reasons not to call competitors include:

1. The contact may be misinterpreted as a probe for proprietary information.

2. It may raise anti-trust issues.

3. Your questions or areas of interest may signal something about your own company's plans or strategies.

Therefore, such calls to competitors should be left to third-party research firms.

Also, and very important, when calling or speaking to a source, always identify yourself and your company affiliation clearly and honestly. (Some companies have explicit rules that employees must always wear nametags with company affiliation visible when they attend conferences and meetings for this reason.) If you are acting for a client, you should state that fact and perhaps a general comment such as "a client in the steel industry" (but never disclose the identity of the client unless you have explicit permission to do so). If you are preparing a multiclient study or working on an article for publication, you should tell the interview subject about these purposes. Surprisingly, each of these purposes will make some people comfortable about talking and freeze up others. For instance, a middle manager may be willing to answer your questions as long as you are NOT going to publish his remarks, while a public relations person may not want to deal with you unless you represent a publication.

Being misled through ignorance or misunderstanding is one thing, and being misled purposefully is another, but the antidote to both is multiple sourcing. Multiple sources of information, whether human or written, increase the reliability and value of information. The need for a second source may be a good reason to make that one additional phone call, or to arrange for one more interview. It will pay off in the long run.

Key resources
in industry information

While not everything is to be found online or over the
telephone, there seems to be an increasing tendency to
think this is so. Sometimes an old-fashioned book is the
best thing to use. We've mentioned the dangers of "standard" lists of anything, but we don't mind living danger-
ously, apparently, so what follows are some favored books
for all kinds of industry information. "All kinds" covers
such things as biographical works, directories of associations, the periodical indexes, and industry overviews,
among others. Many of these are venerable, and in some
cases have been around in one form or another for half a
century or more. Others, like the new **Hoover's Handbook**, is just over a year old, but what a useful corporate
directory it is, and it's reasonably affordable! **Hoover's**
even tries to list peer companies, and often does a fair job
of it. It is quirky. Of course the multi-volume **International
Directory of Company Histories**, as yet unfinished, is
wonderful but expensive. Use it at your library.

Block out some time for yourself and get to know these
works in detail. **Value Line**, too often dismissed as just an
investor's tool, may have invaluable information about the
amount spent on R&D, age of the plants here and abroad,
domestic versus international sales, and so on.

The **Encyclopedia of Associations** is indispensable. Why?
It tells you who to call. It is full of the best networkers in
the business. Association managers have to know the
experts, the industry leaders, because that is who pays
their salaries. And the **Encyclopedia of Associations** lists
most of these people, with a little summary about the trade
associations they work for.

**What can be found where? A subject approach to
industry sources.**

For Information on:	Consult:
Companies	BPI; F&S; NYT
Industies	BPI; F&S; NYT
Articles on market share and market size	F&S; BPI
Articles on individuals	BPI; BI
Citations to information on individuals	BPI; NYT; WWFI
Company histories within an industry	IDCH; HH
Environmental information on industry or company	BPI; F&S; NYT
Identify key companies within an industry	MI; VL
Individual companies within an industry	S&P; VL; F&S; BPI; MI
Industry overview	S&P; USI
Key information resources to an industry	EBI
Market share for companies	S&P
Market share for products in an industry	F&S; BPI
Norms and business ratios	AH; IN; VL

Keys to the Resources Cited

AH	Standard & Poor's Analyst's Handbook
BI	Biographical Index
BPI	Business Periodicals Index
EA	Encyclopedia of Associations
EBI	Encyclopedia of Business Information Sources
F&S	Predicast's F&S Index—U.S. Edition
HH	Hoover's Handbook
IDCH	International Directory of Company Histories
IN	Industry Norms & Key Business Ratios
NYT	New York Times Index
MI	Moody's Investor's Industry Review
S&P	Standard & Poor's Industry Surveys
USI	U.S. Industrial Outlook
VL	Value Line
WWFI	Who's Who in Finance & Industry

Business Periodicals Index

The **Business Periodicals Index** is a cumulative index to English language periodicals. The main body of the index consists of subject entries to business periodical articles arranged in one index. —*from the preface.*

The **Index** analyses over 300 business publications. An H.W. Wilson publication (as is the **Reader's Guide to Periodical Literature**), the index will not index or cover shorter citations or references in the literature, as is done by both the **Predicasts F&S Index** and the **New York Times Index**. The **Index** appears monthly, quarterly, and in a cumulative annual volume. Formerly called the **Industrial Arts Index**, the work has been around for several decades in one form or another.

Use the **Index** to locate articles in the periodical literature on an industry. If you are looking for information from the fifties, the subject headings will often be different from those you are accustomed to. "Strategic" was only used as a military term in the fifties, for example. Professor Porter hadn't yet written on competitive analysis.

Encyclopedia of Associations
The six-volume (at last count) **Encyclopedia** lists national and international associations and organizations under such broad classifications as the following:

- Trade, Business and Commercial Organizations
- Fraternal and Foreign Interest Organizations
- Agricultural Organizations, Commodity Exchanges
- Educational Organizations
- Legal, Government, Public Administration
- Scientific, Engineering and Technical Organizations
- Labor Unions, Associations
- Cultural Organizations
- Chambers of Commerce and Trade Organizations
- Social Welfare and Tourism
- Public Affairs Organizations
- Labor Unions and Federations
- Tourism Organizations

Nearly every product and industry has its own association, which means that there are usually lists of corporate members, pamphlets, and brochures as well as newsletters and magazines for nearly every industry. Magazines and newsletters are listed in the **Encyclopedia,** and can then be sought out in local libraries or through the association itself if materials are hard to locate.

The most common point of access to the **Encyclopedia** is its key word index. For example, the **Encyclopedia** lists over 300 aerospace organizations, from the technical and scientific to the avocational.

Whether you are after the number of golf balls manufactured annually, or after a list of companies in the commercial brush industry, the **Encyclopedia** is a good starting point. It will also tell you the number of members of the association, how often they meet, often where their next meeting will be, the names of any association publications, the director's name, the purpose, and a history of the organization.

Encyclopedia of Business Information Sources

It's always been easy enough to find lists of information resources on an industry, but not until the **Encyclopedia of Business Information Sources** came along could you get a selection of the most important resources for an industry including key periodicals, assoociations, sources of statistics, etc. The **Encyclopedia** proposes to select the most important periodicals or associations in an industry. The **Encyclopedia** is without peer in identifying the key access points to the literature of an industry, and typically breaks these resources into such categories as:

- General Works
- Abstracting and Indexing Services

- Encyclopedias and Dictionaries
- Bibliographies
- Handbooks and Manuals
- Online Databases
- Research Centers and Institutes
- Statistics Sources
- Trade Associations and Professional Societies

Hoover's Handbook: Profiles of 500 Major Corporations
Books attempting to provide company profiles are scarce,
so this entirely new book written by Gary Hoover et al.,
and published by an entirely new enterprise, is good news
for everyone doing business research.

"The core of this book is 542 one-page profiles of major
enterprises, of all types, from around the world. These
profiles are arranged alphabetically. They contain basic
information on the nature of each enterprise, its history, the people who run it, the products or services it
delivers, and its financial performance.

"The profiles are preceded by two other types of
information. First ... we have included some ideas
about how to use and understand the information in
this book. This section includes a basic explanation of
corporations and the way they are measured, recommendations for further reading, and a glossary....

"Following the profiles are four indexes: first, a list of
broad industry groupings and the enterprises in each
group; second, an index of the profiled enterprises by

headquarters location; third, an index of people named in the profiles; and fourth, the main index of the book, which lists all enterprises and products named in the profiles." —*from the preface.*

Industry Norms & Key Business Ratios

Arranged by SIC code, **Industry Norms** contains "typical" balance sheet figures for companies within a certain industry, as well as key ratios. Dollar figures and key ratios are also refined into median and upper and lower quartile. Consult the work itself for the uses and applications of norms and ratios. Knowing the norms and ratios for a company in a certain industry may allow you to deduce a sales range if you have enough other facts at your disposal.

International Directory of Company Histories

Arranged by industry, with two of the proposed five-volume set completed, this work provides detailed corporate histories of 250 companies.

"The International Directory of Company Histories provides accurate and detailed information on the historical development of 1250 of the world's largest and most influential companies. The Directory will consist of five volumes, each containing 250 entries. The first volume covers 10 industries ranging from advertising to drugs. Volumes two through five will cover industries from electronics to utilities.... The companies chosen for inclusion... have met one or both of the following criteria: they have achieved a mini-

mum of 2 billion U.S. dollars in annual sales or
they are a leading influence in a particular industry or geographical location." —*from the preface.*

The **Directory** is definitely international in scope—the first
company in the Aerospace industry is *Airbus Industrie,*
formed in France as a *groupement d'intérêt économique*
(G.I.E.), a form of unlimited partnership commonly used by
vintners and construction projects which involve several
contractors.

Moody's Investor's Industry Review

"Moody's Industry Review is a comprehensive
statistical reference containing key financial
information, operating data, and ratios on approximately 4,000 companies. This valuable
information is arranged by industry, in 145
industry groups..." —*from the introduction.*

The **Review** provides no textual or discursive material on
the companies it includes within an industry. It is, as the
title indicates, a tool for the investor. The multi page
listings consist entirely of a company's place within an
array comprising financial data or various financial ratios.

Each industry covered consists of an alphabetical array of
the major companies within an industry, providing such
information for each company as: its exchange, symbol,
price range, earnings per share, book value, stock holder's
equity, and long term debt.

Following this list, companies are arrayed by such financial and key-ratio data as: revenues, net income, operating profit margin, return on capital, gross plant, net plant, return on net plant, working capital, price-earnings ratio, yield, 12-month price score, and 7-year price score.

Additionally there are special rankings for factors that may be meaningful only in specific industries. For example, in some capital-intensive industries, companies are ranked by size of gross and net plant, return on net plant, and capital expenditures. Other special rankings include such items as Passenger Load Factor (a measure of passenger miles to available seat miles in aviation), and Tobacco Sales as a percentage of Total Sales, in recognition that most tobacco companies are also in a number of other businesses.

New York Times Index

Consider the *New York Times* our national newspaper of record, because it is as close to being that as anything will ever be. Because the *NYT* tends to consider itself as national and international in scope, remember to use it for foreign information. Just as importantly, remember to use it for regional information. If you are after industry information and something important happened in that industry in Detroit, go to the *NYT*. If it was important at all, chances are the newspaper will have it.

Fortunately, the **Times Index** gives the reader an abstract of the article, rather than a title which often enough is not very revealing. For example:

"Union representing 40,000 machinists at Boeing Co. votes to accept three-year contract that offers year-end bonus payments worth thousands of dollars," or, "Singer Com-

pany eliminates about 400 jobs from its aerospace electronics division to cut costs and enhance competitiveness."
Simply scanning the citations of the **Index** can be revealing if you are unfamiliar with an industry.

Predicast's F&S Index—US Edition
Predicast's F&S Indexes (F&S) covers information appearing in hundreds of serial publications. These serials range from newspapers such as the *Wall Street Journal* to trade publications, general business magazines and specialized newsletters. Unlike **Business Periodicals Index, F&S** will note a citation that is no longer than a paragraph in a newspaper. **F&S** also differs in scanning many more publications than **BPI**, including foreign-language issues, and publications that are broader in purpose than a "business magazine."

Predicast's F&S Indexes are issued monthly, quarterly and annually. Each issue is arranged in two sections:

1. Company information, arranged alphabetically in the white pages.

2. Industry or product information, arranged by SIC number, in the colored pages.

The introductory material in each volume includes Predicast's SIC codes and a listing of all the publications indexed by **F&S**. Often valuable corporate or industry information can be gleaned by glancing at **F&S**. For example:

*   "Boeing—organizational history—*Forbes* 07/13/87 p. 164."

- "Boeing—aims to cut at least 80% of $1.4 billion loss from wasted resources in 1986."

- "Boeing—won total of $3.5 billion in defense contracts in Fy 1986, *WSJ* 03/11/87 p. 17."

- "US civil aircraft exports rise to $13.7 billion in 1986 vs. $12.3 billion in 1985, *IntAil* 08/12/87 p. 5."

Special Issues Index

A multi-volume set that describes which "special" issues of business and trade publications regularly cover certain industries. In addition **Special Issues** also lists separately published studies of an industry. This publication has reached an age of ten years, as of 1992, which is old for such a work. Nonetheless, it is the only title that tackles this task, and much of the information may still be usable.

Standard & Poor's Analyst's Handbook

The Analyst's Handbook provides "a unique set of analytical tools: selected income account and balance sheet items and related ratios as applied to the S&P industry group stock price indexes from 1957 to date. These data are kept up to date quarterly, to the extent that quarterly information is available, through the monthly supplement in the envelope at the end of this volume."

Each page of industry group data lists those companies that have been used in creating the data, and the times for which they were included. Boeing has been included in these data from November 3, 1934 to date, for example.

Standard & Poor's Industry Surveys

The opening paragraph under "Aerospace Industry Fundamentals" notes in part:

> "The aerospace industry is characterized by a high degree of concentration, formidable barriers to new entrants, labor & capital-intensiveness, and a marketing environment permeated by politics. The US aerospace industry leads world markets and has historically led all domestic industries in quantity of exports."

Unlike the U.S. Department of Commerce's **Outlook, S&P Industry Surveys** often goes into detail about the performance of key companies in an industry. For example:

> "McDonnell Douglas appears to have settled into a niche at about 16% of orders... During 1987, it has received orders for 73 MD-80's, and three DC-10's, compared to a total of 64 aircraft a year ago. The company's new entry into the long-range field, the MD-11, a derivative of the DC-10, received no new orders for the model during 1987..."

Tables include:

- Aerospace Sales by Customer
- Shipments of Complete Civilian Aircraft
- Civil Transport Aircraft Backlog
- General Aviation Shipments
- Significant Aerospace Industry Statistics
- Aerospace Employment

- DOD Outlays by Function (NASA, etc.)
- Aerospace Trade Balance
- Leading Military Prime Contractors

U.S. Department of Commerce Publications

- Annual Survey of Manufacturers
- Census of Manufacturers
- Census of Retail Trade
- Census of Selected Service Industries
- Census of Wholesale Trade
- Statistical Abstract of the U.S.—Annual

U.S. Industrial Outlook Handbook

For an orientation to a particular industry you might begin by consulting the **U.S. Industrial Outlook Handbook**. It is an annual produced by the U.S. Department of Commerce. Each article is written and signed by a government specialist in the field.

The **Outlook's** chapter on the Aerospace industry begins with the following paragraph:

> "The US aerospace industry, a national and
> global leader, is a critical element of the U.S.
> economy. In 1990, aerospace ranked sixth in
> value of shipments and tenth in employment
> among all U.S. industries. More important,
> aerospace is the nation's leading exporter, send-
> ing abroad products worth $38 billion in 1990 to

135 countries around the world. Aerospace produces the largest trade surplus of any U.S. industry ($26 billion in 1990), which significantly reduces the nation's merchandise trade deficit. The aerospace industry also accounts for more than 25 percent of all the nation's research and development expenditures, making it the technology leader in this country." —*U.S. Industrial Outlook '92*

Tables and charts in this section include:

1. Trends and Forecasts: Aerospace (SIC 372, 376)

2. U.S. Aerospace Industry: Military and Civil Sector Shares of Shipments/Backlog

3. Aerospace Industry Profits as a Percent of Sales

4. U.S. Trade Patterns in 1990: Aerospace

5. U.S. Aerospace Trade with the World, 1980-1992

6. U.S. Exports of Aerospace Vehicles & Equipment, 1988-92

7. U.S. Imports of Aerospace Vehicles and Equipment, 1988-92

8. Trends and Forecasts: Aircraft

9. Shipments of Complete U.S. Aircraft, 1971-92

Amply supplemented with tables and graphs, each article discusses the year's performance, and will often go back 10 years in tabular comparisons for various measures of production. **Outlook** goes into detail about unit shipments; factors influencing sales; recent trends driving the industry; segment data; materials costs, and so on.

The **Outlook** also, as the title indicates, projects the industry's performance into the near future. Appended to each article is a list of such other sources of information as industry newsletters, recent articles and magazines.

You will seldom find competing companies ranked or compared in the **Outlook**; however, for highly centralized industries such as aerospace, it will discuss individual companies and orders for particular aircraft. Perhaps it is inevitable for this to happen in an industry in which two companies manufacture 85% of all commercial aircraft. For more fragmented industries, **Standard & Poor's Industry Surveys** is a good source for the makeup of an industry and for a discussion of companies within that industry.

Unfortunately the Department of Commerce has chosen to eliminate certain industries for reasons that are as yet unclear, but are stated as "largely budgetary in nature". The 1992 **Outlook** issue no longer covers rigid containers, for example, an omission deeply felt by those doing industry analysis in metal, glass, plastic or cardboard packaging.

Value Line Investment Survey
Value Line is primarily an investor's tool, but it also has uses for those seeking competitive intelligence. The **Survey** gives stock performance of companies within 70 industries over a period of ten years or so, and also tracks certain performance ratios. In addition, in the "business" section for each company, line-of-business or segment data is often provided, as well as the percentage of business here and abroad. For example, under Boeing, the business section notes:

"U.S. Government business: 32 percent of total sales; exports: 45 percent; research and development: 5.4 percent; labor costs: 33 percent; 1987 depreciation rate: 8.7 percent; estimated plant age: 6 years ..."

International business:
hard copy resources

International information is at a premium now, and good
sources for it are especially valuable. Europe is unifying,
and the power of that new entity could be awesome. Japan
and the Pacific Rim countries mean big business as well.
Decision makers are realizing that they must look beyond
the U. S. for business opportunities — and threats. International is another word for the great globe itself, and that
means more sources, and more diversity of resources, than
those covering just U.S. businesses. These is a surprising
depth of both historical and current information in these
works.

Here is a basic list, divided by categories:

- **directories**
- **statistical works**
- **encyclopedias/handbooks/surveys**, and
- **atlases**

Directories
**America's Corporate Families and International
Affiliates**
   Dun & Bradstreet. Annual.

This directory lists "multinational corporate families
having at least one U.S. family member and at least one
elsewhere."—*from the introduction.*

Address, annual sales estimate, number of employees,
subsidiaries, and officers are given.

Directory of American Firms Operating in Foreign Countries
Uniworld Business Publications

Section I is an alphabetical listing of American companies which gives address, type of business, and countries in which the company operates. Section II lists companies by country of operation.

Directory of Foreign Firms Operating in the United States
Uniworld Business Publications

Part 1 is arranged by country with companies listed alphabetically. For each company the address and principal industry of the U.S. company and the name of its foreign parent company are given. Part 2 lists foreign parent companies in alphabetical order and gives American subsidiaries or affiliates. Part 3 is an alphabetical listing of U.S. subsidiaries, branches or affiliates of foreign firms. For each, the foreign parent company is listed.

Directory of Foreign Manufacturers in the United States
by Arpan, Jeffrey & D.A. Rickes.
Georgia State University.

Lists manufacturers with at least 10% foreign ownership, either directly or indirectly. For each company, address, parent company and its location or address, product category, and SIC is given. Indexed by state, parent company's name and country, and SIC number.

Europe's 15,000 Largest Companies
Dun & Bradstreet. Annual.

Includes industrial, trading and transportation companies, banks, insurance and advertising agencies. Companies are ranked in their category according to sales. Information given includes sales, number of employees and shareholders, assets, profits, etc.

International Directory of Corporate Affiliations: "Who Owns Whom"
National Register Publishing Co. Annual.

> "Designed to give an in-depth view of major multinational companies, subsidiaries and affiliates... Contains companies listed in the New York and American stock exchanges, the Fortune 1000, as well as those whose stock is traded over the counter, and many that are privately owned."
> —*From the section, "Facts you should know about this directory."*

Section 1 is an alphabetical list of parent companies, divisions, subsidiaries, etc. Section 2 is an alphabetical listing of foreign parent companies with their divisions, subsidiaries, affiliates, etc.; Section 3 lists U.S. companies with foreign holdings.

Major Companies of the Arab World
Graham & Trotman. Annual

"Companies are listed alphabetically by country... The end of the book contains three cross-referenced indexes: 1) an alphabetical listing of all companies contained in Major Companies of the Arab World; 2) an alphabetical listing of all companies included in each country section; and 3) a business activity index of all listed companies subdivided by type of business."

Major Companies of the Far East
Volume 1: South East Asia
Graham & Trotman. Annual

"The companies listed have been selected on the grounds of the size of their sales volume or balance sheet of their importance to the business environment of the country in which they are based." Companies are listed alphabetically within each country. The index includes three cross-reference indexes which list all companies alphabetically, list them alphabetically by country, and list them as they are arranged by type of business or product.

Major Companies of the Far East
Volume 2: East Asia
Graham & Trotman. Annual

"The companies listed have been selected on the grounds of the size of their sales volume or balance sheet or their importance to the business environment of the country in which they are based." Alphabetical arrangement by country. The index includes three cross-reference indexes which list all companies alphabetically, list them alphabetically by country, and list them by type of business or product.

Moody's International Manual
Dun & Bradstreet. Annual with supplements.

Contains "financial and business information on more than 5,200 major corporations and national and supranational institutions in 100 countries. Corporate information contained includes company history, description of business and property, financial statements, management, debt, capital, and other key data. A number of companies have expanded descriptions which provide a more in-depth picture of corporate operations. National economic data is also included."—*from the introduction.*

Principal International Businesses
Dun & Bradstreet. Annual.

Lists companies alphabetically by country, by name of company and by SIC number. For each, the following information is given: Dun's number, address, sales, number of employees, SIC number, line of business, chief officer. For subsidiaries, the name of the parent company is given.

Worldwide Chamber of Commerce Directory
Worldwide Chamber of Commerce Directory, Inc.

In addition to U.S. Chambers of Commerce, this work also lists:

- State Boards of Tourism
- Convention and Visitors Bureaus
- Canadian Chambers of Commerce
- Mexican Chambers of Commerce
- Various foreign Chambers

Statistical Works
Balance of Payments Statistics
International Monetary Fund. Annual.

Gives statistics, covering a five-year period, for over 100 countries, including capital, reserve goods, services.

Caribbean Basin to the Year 2000:
Demographic, Economic and Resource-Use Trends in Seventeen Countries
Graham, Norman A. & Keith L. Edwards.
Westview Press.

Indexes of economic performance for the major industrial countries are given in chart and tabular form.

Consumer Price Indices: Sources and Methods and Historical Statistics
Organization for Economic Cooperation and Development (OECD).

Contains historical statistics for a 20-year period, as well as a summary of the essential features of the indices and their methods of calculation.

Demographic Yearbook
United Nations. Annual.

For over two hundred countries or areas throughout the world statistics for population trends, births, deaths, marriages and divorces are broken down by age and sex, national and/or ethnic composition, language and religion. Statistics are also given for geographic, educational and economic characteristics of the population.

European Historical Statistics: 1750-1970
Mitchell, B.R.
Columbia University Press.

Statistics are given for the following topics: climate, population and vital statistics, labor force, agriculture, industry, external trade, transport and communications, finance, prices, education.

European Marketing Data and Statistics
Euromonitor Publications.

> "European Marketing Data and Statistics is a compendium of statistical information on the countries of Western and Eastern Europe. Published annually, it provides a wealth of detailed and up-to-date statistical information relevant to international market planning... The handbook is more fully indexed than previous editions and there is a guide to sources used in the compilation."—*from the introduction.*

Figures given cover populations, employment, production, trade, economy, standard of living, consumption, market sizes, retailing, consumer expenditure, housing and households, health and education, travel and tourism.

International Financial Statistics Yearbook
International Monetary Fund. Annual.

Reports data, starting in 1951, for most countries. Includes exchange rates, international liquidity, money and banking, international trade, prices, production, government finances, interest rates, etc. Updated monthly by the journal International Financial Statistics.

International Historical Statistics—Africa and Asia
  Mitchell, B.R.
  New York University Press.

This compendium lists:

- Annual Precipitation by country from 1886 to 1975
- Deaths of Infants under One Year Old Per 1,000 Births
- Number of Industrial Disputes
- Indices of Wages or Earnings
- Output of Citrus Fruits (in thousand metric tons)
- Numbers of Livestock (in thousands)
- Output of Copper Ore

Main Economic Indicators: Historical Statistics, 1960-1979
  Organization for Economic Cooperation and Development (OECD).

Arranged in chapters by country, statistics for the years 1960-1979 include gross national product, real domestic product, manufacturing, construction, prices, labor and wages, interest rates, foreign trade, etc.

Statistical Yearbook
  United Nations. Annual.

For all U.N. member countries, statistical data is given on economic performance and productivity, relative level of economic development, output of major industries, agriculture and transportation, energy, trade, etc. Updated and supplemented by the Monthly Bulletin of Statistics.

World Development Report
The World Bank. Annual.

Assesses economic development issues and the "World Development Indicators" section gives "selected social and economic data for more than a hundred countries."—*from the foreword.*

World in Figures
G.K. Hall & Company

For each country, in two colors of ink, this book provides a wealth of tabular information. It is a marvel of concise reporting, and probably the first place to look for that elusive fact on a country.

> "Provides detailed figures on each country in the world, and also on the relative importance of countries of the world under various subject headings."—*from the introduction.*

Yearbook of International Trade Statistics
United Nations. Annual.

Export and import figures are given for member nations of SITC (Standard International Trade Classification) code. The scope of the data included covers several years and the latest years available are shown for each country.

Yearbook of Labor Statistics
International Labor Office. Annual.

Present summaries of the principal labor statistics for over 150 countries or territories. Whenever possible, the data covers the last ten years.

Encyclopedias, Handbooks,and Surveys
Doing Business In France (or Germany, or...)
   Price Waterhouse.

An ongoing series, with each volume devoted to a different country. The Prefatory Note indicates at which point in time the material was collected. Chapters on the **Doing Business in France** volume, include: France–a Profile; Business Climate; Foreign Investment and Trade Opportunities; Investment Incentives; Restrictions on Foreign Investment; Regulatory Environment; Banking and Finance; Exporting to France; Business Entities; Labor Relations and Social Security; Audit Requirements and Practices; Tax System; Tax Administration, etc. With EC-1992 drawing closer, European countries are changing their trade regulations with considerable speed. Even a book current to last month would need to be checked against the most recent EC regulations and the country's changing rules and regulations.

Economic and Social Survey of Asia and the Pacific 1989
   United Nations. Economic and Social Commission for Asia.

"A survey of recent economic and social development in the region ... [and] an analysis of international trade, trade policies and development in the countries of the region."

Economic Survey of Europe in 1988-1989
   United Nations. Economic Commission for Europe.

Surveys the economic situation of Europe including Eastern Europe and the Soviet Union. Industrial production and demand, foreign trade, wages and prices, and employment are some of the topics covered. Charts and statistical tables supplement the text.

Economics of the Arabian Gulf:
A Statistical Source Book
by Kubursi, Atif.
Croom Helm Ltd.

Encyclopedia of the Third World, Third Edition
by George Thomas Kurian
Facts On File, Inc.
Oxford, England

This revision covers the period from January 1, 1981 to June 1, 1986, a relatively quiet time for the third world, according to the preface. "In 1984 the population of the Third World (excluding China) reached 2.354 billion, or slightly over 52% of the global population for that year... The Gross Domestic Product (GDP) of the Third World reached $2.111 trillion for 1980 (compared to $3.275 trillion for the United States)."

Europa Year Book
Europa Publications. Annual.

This two-volume encyclopedia provides information on international organizations and countries throughout the world. Information for each country includes: history, government, economic affairs, education, tourism, judicial system, communication and transportation, etc.

European Community:
A Guide for Business and Government
by Morris, Brian, et al.
Indiana University Press.

Alphabetical arrangement includes descriptions of community institutions, industrial and trade unions, consumer organizations, etc.

Foreign Commerce Handbook
  by Maffrey, Ann Dwyer.
  Chamber of Commerce of the United States.

Handy guide to agencies and organizations that offer
international business and foreign trade services. Also
provides descriptions of key subjects.

International Banking Hand Book
  Dow Jones-Irwin.

Organized around the major issues and functions involved
in international banking. There are chapters on topics such
as Eurocurrency market; country risk analysis—economic
and non-economic factors; international leasing, expansion
of foreign banks in the U.S. All chapters are written by
experts in the field.

International Finance Handbook
  John Wiley & Sons.

Designed for the non-specialist, the book deals with practical problems of international finance. It is divided into
several major parts: foreign exchange markets,
Eurocurrency markets, national banking, money and bond
markets, international bond markets, international equity
markets, special financing techniques and sources and
management international finance.

Markets of Asia Pacific: People's Republic of China
  by Chen, Edward, and Steve Chin.
  Facts on File, Inc.

Charts and text describe the economic and political background, people, household income expenditure, agriculture and industry, financial structure, foreign and domestic trade to provide an overview of the market in China.

Statesman's Year Book
St. Martin's Press. Annual.

Provides concise information on the countries of the world. Topics covered include: constitution and government, area, population, religion, state finance, defense, production and industry, agriculture, commerce, banking and credit, money, etc.

Third World Economic Handbook
by Sinclair, Stuart.
Euromonitor Publications.

"The chief purpose of this book is to introduce the main countries of this group, offering some insights into their recent and likely future prospects as markets for exporters, investors and indeed as sources for the importer."

Third World Resource Directory: A Guide to Organizations & Publications
Fenton, Thomas P., ed.
Orbis Books.

> "The organizations listed here have been set up by people who have dedicated themselves to finding out how the powers-that-be in this country have increased the misery in the Third World... It is a guide to organizations that systematically pore over reports of congressional hearings, carefully analyze corporate and government documents, meticulously monitor the press, and, in general, make it their business to gather, study and disseminate this critical information."—*from the foreword.*

World Bank Annual Report
World Bank. Annual.

Includes economic assessments of regions of the world, such as Western Africa and South Africa, with special attention to some countries.

World Economic Outlook
International Monetary Fund
Washington, D.C.

"The projections and analysis contained in the World Economic Outlook are the product of a comprehensive interdepartmental review of world economic developments by the staff of the International Monetary Fund." Originally published annually, now (since 1984) published semi-annually.

World Economic Survey
United Nations. Annual.

An annual survey of current trends and policies in the world economy, developing countries, centrally planned economies and some major developed market economies.

Atlases
Asian Market Atlas
Business International.

Through maps, charts and graphs: (1) compares the ASIA/PACIFIC area to rest of world, (2) examines individual countries in this area relative to the region as a whole, (3) and describes countries on an individual basis.

Atlas of ECC Affairs
  by Hudson, Ray, et al.
  Methuen.

Describes "in maps and words recent trends, current problems, future prospects" of the European Economic Community.

Rand McNally Commercial Atlas & Marketing Guide
  Rand McNally. Annual.

The last section of this commonly available atlas contains maps and material on foreign countries. Included are population data, time zones, airline and steamship distances, elevations for world cities, a list of the world's largest metropolitan areas. An under-used resource with valuable international information.

Industry analysis and
issues studies

Much competitive intelligence work focuses on companies
or products, but often it is useful to pull back for a wider
view. This could be a hard look at an industry or industry
segment, or it could involve the impact (e.g., environmental regulation) on a competitive situation.

Industry studies are major projects, often involving weeks
or months of work—and organizing piles of information
from many sources, some hard-won. They usually start
from a base of knowledge, but sometimes (and sometimes
usefully) they can begin at the very beginning, with the
researcher knowing nothing at all about the industry to be
studied.

Whatever the starting point on the learning curve, the first
step is planning:

> *What essential elements of information are required?*
>
> *What sources will be used to find them?*

A comprehensive industry study should include sections
on:

- the size, growth rate, market characteristics and
  trends of the industry
- profiles of the companies that are major players
  (including sales, market share, and strategic position
  when obtainable)
- product lines and substitute products (current and
  potential)

- suppliers to the industry
- principal customers for the industry's products
- manufacturing and distribution technologies/ patterns
- major innovations and new technologies
- social and economic conditions as they affect the industry

A tailored or custom industry study may include only a few of these categories, and focus on them in some depth.

An industry study can present a considerable challenge. One study we were asked to do involved an obscure industry segment about which little had been written. Aggregated industry data had no separate breakout for this segment. In short, little pre-existing information was available. The study had to be built almost entirely from over 100 interviews with knowledgeable individuals.

How to begin? It is a good rule just to dive into research right away and get into the interviewing phase (primary research) as early as possible. Once information starts to accumulate, strategies begin to take form to get the precise information needed and fill in the gaps.

At some point about a third of the way into the project, the research team should take a step back and ask:

What objectives have been met easily in the early stages of the project?

What resources will be needed to get the additional essential information?

Even though specific planning for information collection may need to wait until the project is underway, it is always necessary to have a clear overall goal for the study. First determine what this study is to be used for. If there is no current or forseeable use, perhaps there should be no study. The goals should to be clear to all concerned parties.

Once you begin to run into referrals to sources you have already consulted, you will know you are nearing the end of the collection phase. Now is the time to refine your analysis and begin writing the final report. In terms of allocating time, a good rule is: two-thirds of the allotted time should go to collection and analysis, while the final third is devoted to writing the report. (Nevertheless, collection of information should continue up to the time the report is delivered and perhaps beyond, even though the time spent on collection will have diminished to a small percentage of the effort.)

A typical scenario is a three-month project where the first two months involve collection and analysis, with analysis growing more important as time moves along and information piles up. Then the final month is spent putting the report into final form, writing up the results and formatting a smoothly professional document. The final report may leave some questions unanswered, but it should represent a sound understanding of the industry.

The study's goals determine what particular elements of information are included. A research team must avoid the trap of creating a study that is more extensive than the goals. Doing more than is required is a sure road to the dusty shelves of the archives.

One U. S. company launched a competitive monitoring program in the early 1980s and hired a highly credentialed individual to run it. This research effort produced filing cabinet after filing cabinet full of data, and shelf after shelf full of unread studies. The archives ended up in a disused corridor, and the head of the research team ended up outside the company. The net result was a lot of expense and not much value for the company. Competitive studies must be clearly relevant and actionable or they will be ignored.

Doing an industry study is an endurance run, not a sprint. It is punctuated by periods of discouragement. It also requires the ability to see patterns and make meaningful connections in large masses of information, between seemingly unrelated facts. One of the essential tasks is to make sense out of the clutter, to draw clarity out of complexity.

The various types of data begin to work together as you get into the study. Aggregate industry data provides a framework. The structure of that framework becomes clearer as you place individual pieces of information within it.

As the financial and organizational data build, the dynamics of the industry should begin to "seep" into your mind, until you are living with the picture of the industry that is emerging. Then some interesting things will begin to come into focus. There may be a better way of distributing products that stands out from the data. Or it may become clear what competitive advantages an individual competitor may have and how to cope with them.

As long as industry studies make contributions that support profitability, they will pay their way.

One useful subset of industry studies is issues studies. These reports look at how one issue, e.g., environmental regulation, may affect a company or market segment. What is the best way to address the issue in question, and how will the social expression of the issue develop in the future? What strategies are available to meet the demands of those future developments?

Issues studies have more general frames of reference, but they must also have real relevance to profitability. The power of any idea derives not only from the idea itself but from the time, place and circumstances that make it flourish.

A case study in public document access: an FTC hearing and the glass packaging industry

The quest for information

And so the prince returned from the Valley of
Promise and sorrowfully made his way back to the
king, his father, for he had failed in his first quest
and was sorely afraid he would never be permitted to make another.

"Mercy, Father," he cried, falling on one knee and
reluctantly holding forth his sword. "I am not to
blame. The evil gatekeeper put me on the wrong
road, and I lost my horse. Then the forest people
drugged me with wine, and I lost my strength.
The very page you gave me was in the service of
the dragon. The dragon himself was unrecognizable. And the maiden proved, in sooth, to be no
maiden. Surely such hazards are beyond all
reason. The contest was not fair."

"It never is," said the king, taking his sword.

A Packet of Fairy Tales[23]
Anon.

A competitive intelligence firm, Kockerham Associates,
was asked to study the rigid container industry in the
United States by the Benson Packaging Company, a multi-
national firm operating solely in the tin and steel can
business. Benson's Vice President for Business Development indicated that Benson Packaging planned to
diversify, to spread both the risks and opportunities

arising from market shifts in kinds of packaging, and
wanted a project that would fully detail the opportunities
and risks in such diversification.

Before launching into the information gathering phase of
the research, the project director got together with those
who would be working on the project and discussed the
project in terms of goals and research activities. Each
member of the team had a copy of the contract and an
expanded explanation of the scope of the project prepared
by the project manager.

The project manager had already reached the bottom of
the U-shaped curve on this project, because a great deal of
the information looked more than difficult—it looked like
the sort of material most packaging companies would
consider closely-held and strategic and all the other terms
a company uses when it wants to play its cards close-to-
the-vest. He could not quite imagine how major parts of
the project would be accomplished, and looked forward to
sharing his despair with his colleagues.

The scope of the packaging study

1. Who are the U.S. competitors in the major types of
   rigid packaging?

   - Steel and tin cans
   - Aluminum cans
   - Glass bottles and jars
   - Plastic bottles jars and tubs

2. Describe major competitors by industry in terms of market share, sales, recent capitalization, customer base, number and location of plants, age of equipment, type of equipment in use (particularly for glass) type and age and utilization of furnaces, technological capabilities, patents held, and region of distribution.

3. Describe each industry (packaging type) in terms of product volume for prior ten years, projected volume/sales for two years. Where possible break out sales by market and product segment.

4. Detail the direct and indirect costs of entering each of these industries.

5. What is the nature of international sales in each industry? Who is importing and exporting to which markets?

6. How had acquisitions impacted on the various industries? What kinds of acquisitions were done cross-nationally? Look at the impact of domestic and international acquisitions on corporate performance. Did the acquisition "work better" if it involved two different kinds of packaging, or if it was in the same business?

7. How do environmental issues impact on each industry? What has the impact been in the recent past, and what is it now? What stage of maturity has each industry reached in terms of recycling infrastructure. What impending and future environmental issues will impact on sales?

The environment and packaging

The client was particularly alive to environmental issues, not just because he was in metal and packaging manufacture, but also because aluminum can manufacturers were forced to deal with aluminum recycling and environmental issues some twenty years ago with the introduction of the pop-top can, and by dealing with it promptly and effectively had stolen major share in the beverage segment from steel and glass. Plastic for a time was stealing share from steel, glass and aluminum in a variety of product categories.

The client had also noted that in Germany steel cans dominate aluminum packaging by an 80/20 ratio, exactly the opposite of the U.S., where aluminum now dominates steel by an 80/20 ratio. He noted that a steel can could be more easily and cheaply recycled, melted down and manufactured than an aluminum can. "But we were all asleep at the switch 20 years ago when the aluminum can was struggling for survival and in the process building an environmental infrastructure that we would love to have right now ourselves." This suggested to him that environmental issues had directly changed the production of packaging far more deeply than usually thought. Usually when we think of environmental issues having an impact on an industry we think of additional overhead and higher manufacturing costs, and not about environmental issues reshaping the industry. For these reasons the client wanted particular emphasis placed on research in steel vs. aluminum packaging and the issue of environmental forces playing on production both here and in major European countries. He was also aware, and wanted us to be aware, that steel production had always been strong in Germany.

8. What new or emerging technologies would impact on the various types of packaging? How much packaging is being driven by microwave oven ownership? What impact is the shelf-stable (gas-pack) package having on more traditional packaging? Why has it been less successful in America than in Europe?

After the meeting, during which everyone agreed that much of the information their client wanted was going to be near-to-impossible to get, but that somehow they would probably get it, the project manager made the initial assignments.

The project was initially broken down by types of agencies or media to be accessed, rather than subject or industry. Later, following the initial inquiries and the first flurry of information, the team would sit down again and discuss the project in terms of availability of information and probable points of access to further investigation. Then the project would be broken out by subject, and reassigned by the project manager.

Kockerham Associates did database searches on the packaging industry, looking for market conditions, major players, and mergers and acquisitions within the past ten years, and at the same time, they initiated phone calls to the Glass Packaging Institute, a plastic container association and to the packaging industry specialist for the U.S. Industrial Outlook. One of the team members had a friend who was formerly with the EPA, and who was now setting up shop in the consulting business. He was called.

All the approaches were productive in one way or another, but there was still no serious light at the end of the tunnel. One of the database searches pulled a full text article from *Packaging Week*[24] detailing world market-share for packaging companies. This was considered a minor coup, because market share is one of the most difficult things to nail down.

Everyone talks about market share a great deal in business research, and sometimes you can find something close to viable market share on an industry, but it is usually hard to get. The difficulty with most market-share tables one finds is that they aren't broken out by market segment. That is, almost no two packaging companies (or any other kind of company) are alike in their product lines. Some do mostly aluminum, but do some steel; some do all steel, some do some steel and a little aluminum; some do glass, plastic, steel and aluminum and some metal and plastic caps as well. Some do ultra-thin light-wall cans and high-technology closures and caps. One company might hold a number of patents and commonly make heavy research and development efforts. Company A might be doing 43 million in steel can sales for the paint and hardware business, and company B might be doing 43 million in steel can sales for the canned peas. Comparing the two you would see two companies with $43 million in steel can sales, but the two companies are not competitors—all one sees is the potential to compete.

Many market-share tables, from this perspective, compare apples and oranges. If you are an investor, mixing apples and oranges may not be important, but if you are a manufacturer or researcher trying to fully understand the dynamics of the packaging industry, comparing apples and oranges can be frustrating.

Table: Estimated overall market shares in world packaging, 1988

Ranking	Company	Headquarters Country	Share FFr bn
1	Pechiney	France	32.0
2	Toyo Seikan	Japan	31.4
3	CMB Packaging	UK/France	24.1
4	Tetra Pak	Sweden	24.0
5	Owens Ilinois	US	21.9
6	Crown	US	21.5
7	Continental Can	US	11.2
8	PLM	Sweden	6.1
9	BSN	France	5.6
10	Lawson Mardon	Canada	4.9

Source: *Packaging Week*, June 6, 1990.

Table: Market shares in European metal packaging, 1988

Producer	Food	Beverage
CMB Packaging	35%	22%
Continental Can	7%	24%
Pechiney	10%	39%
Others	48%	15%

Source: *Packaging Week*, June 6, 1990.

From an Investext search they retrieved an analyst's report on the U.S. packaging industry that gave production figures on glass, plastic and metal packaging (steel and aluminum) for ten years.

The **U.S. Industrial Outlook** also had a wealth of information on the industry, including near-term projections by type of packaging. As usual, the **Outlook** article was signed by the industry specialist who wrote the piece, and his Washington telephone number was included. (Sadly, in 1992, the government decided to discontinue packaging industry analysis in the **Outlook**.)

In a phone conversation, the **Outlook** packaging specialist told Kockerham that Owens-Illinois, a Toledo, Ohio, glass and plastic container company, had recently undertaken an acquisition of Brockway Glass, a Florida packaging company in the same markets. The FTC had intervened, and there had been a hearing. He understood the FTC had issued a report based on the hearing, and had heard it was a good source of information.

The FTC had decided to intervene with a temporary restraining order in this acquisition because the impending merger of these two companies would create a mega-firm with just under 38% market share in glass packaging, and possibly change the nature of competition across a number of packaging types. It would also create a company with primary market-share in rigid plastic containers, though this seemed a less important issue than glass packaging. (This may have been in part because market share is more easily built or bought in plastic containers than in glass containers, where facilities, glass furnaces, and blow-molding equipment are more expensive.)

The document was titled, **Federal Trade Commission v. Owens-Illinois, Inc., et al., & Brockway, Inc.** (681 F. Supp. 27.) One of the tables listed the glass companies in the U.S., the number of plants operated by each company, market share and sales.

Selected glass producers: 1986			
Company	Number of plants	'86 Sales	Share
Anchor/Diam. B.	23	$1,079	23.7%
Owens-Illinois	14	1,033	22.7
Brockway	11	681	15.0
Ball-InCon	13	520	11.4
Triangle	8	375	8.2
Kerr	4	140	3.1
Gallo	1	140	3.1
Latchford	2	100	2.2
Wheaton	2	100	2.2
Miller	1	75	1.7
Liberty	1	69	1.5
Industrial (KKR/Tropicana)	1	50	1.1
Coors	1	50	1.1
Glenshaw	1	49	1.1
Anchor-Hocking (CL)	1	30	.7
Hillsboro	1	21	.5
Arkansas	1	16	.4
Leone	1	13	.3
Source: *FTC v. Owens-Illinois, (681, F. Sup. 27.)*			

The document described the struggle for survival in the marketplace between glass, metal, plastic and paper packaging. It chose a number of market segments in packaging (baby food, pickles, liquor, etc.) and discussed the varieties of packaging and their losses or gains over twenty years. Expert testimony from both sides revealed the changes the industry had undergone.

> Owens-Illinois had 22.2% of the furnace capacity in 1986, Brockway had 14.9%. Thus, at the time of the merger, Owens-Illinois/Brockway controlled 37% of the glass industry's furnace capacity. The FTC argued that an industry operating at very high capacity has enhanced opportunities for collusion.

> Owens-Illinois estimates that additional capacity available on a short-term basis from existing facilities throughout the industry might be as high as 26%. Capacity committed to glass will also be freed with the continuing conversion of major products from glass to plastic. For example, pourable dressings, which are converting to plastic, account for 150,000 tons of glass per year, or approximately the size of the market for glass pickle containers. The complete conversion of peanut butter by mid-1988 to plastic would also release about 150,000 tons of capacity, about the size of the jam and jelly glass container market. Likewise, if all distillers followed Seagram's lead and converted 1.75-liter liquor containers to plastic, an additional 200,000 tons of capacity would be freed, bigger than the spaghetti sauce glass container industry and almost the size of the baby food glass jar market.

Glass manufacturers' furnace capacity utilization	
Manufacturer	**Capacity Utilization**
Anchor	92%
Anchor-Hocking	90
Arkansas	86
Ball-InCon	86
Brockway	90
Columbine (Coors)	90
Gallo	102*
Glenshaw	87
Industrial (Tropicana)	95
Kerr	91
Latchford	90
Liberty	92
Miller	100
Owens-Illinois	96
Triangle	93
Wheaton	89
Total industry average	92

* Glass plants can be run in excess of 100% capacity by operating during holidays and using "electric boosting."

Source: *FTC v. Owens-Illinois, (681, F. Sup. 27.)*

Glass container companies' capital expenditures	
Company	Capital Expenditures
Owens-Illinois	$80-90 million per year average
Brockway	$47 million per year average
Anchor Glass	$40 million in 1986
Diamond-Bathurst	$40 million in 1986
Liberty Glass	$40 million per year average
Ball-InCon	$24 million in 1986
Foster Forbes	$12 million per year average
Kerr	$5 million per year average
Wheaton Glass	$5 million per year average
Source: FTC v. Owens-Illinois, (681, F. Sup. 27.)	

These excerpts suggest the kind of information that can sometimes be found through a wide range of digging—in this case it was a government industry expert who had heard about a hearing with the FTC, but our experience suggests that if we had not heard about it from one source, another would have brought it up.Simply asking questions of people among such far-flung enterprises as associations, industry, private consultancies and government agencies assures that important information sources, like the FTC hearing, do not remain hidden.

Kockerham Associates' research on the rigid container business was still in its formative stages, but the hearing would prove to be a gold mine of competitive information throughout the course of the investigation.

The hearing document listed expert witnesses on both sides of the question, witnesses who could be telephoned about related issues or about issues brought up during the hearing that needed clarification.

Much of the information spelled out in the course of the hearing would, under normal circumstances, be considered private or privileged. A number of the glass packaging companies (Latchford, Leone and Wheaton to name three) are privately held companies that wouldn't consider releasing information on sales, plant expenditures, market share or furnace capacity utilization to the view of the public and, more importantly, their competition. One imagines that even the big public glass packaging companies would find many of the disclosures distasteful.

But giving up confidential information to a government inquiry such as the FTC anti-trust hearing was not optional for the companies operating within the industry (the hearing is ostensibly being held, after all, to protect the competitive interests of their industry), and once the testimony and the operational and financial data from industry participants is spelled out and incorporated into a public document, what was once confidential closely held strategic information becomes common currency, and grist for the competitive intelligence researcher's mill.

---

[23]   Robert Glynn Kelly, **A Lament for Barney Stone**, New York, NY, Holt, Rinehart & Winston, 1961, p. 205.

[24]   Tim Rothwell, "Global Warning," *Packaging Week*, v. 6, June 6, 1990, p. 17-19.

Due diligence:
getting it done

> Due Dil´-i-gence
> "Such a measure of prudence, activity or assiduity, as
> is properly to be expected from, and ordinarily
> exercised by, a reasonable and prudent man..."
> **Black's Law Dictionary**

Shortly after Bill Stewart bought his packaging company, it
and he were named in a class-action hazardous waste suit.
Given his products and manufacturing processes, Stewart
didn't even see a potential for hazardous waste. The suit
claimed that the water table under nearby homes had been
polluted years earlier by illegal waste disposal. Stewart
would learn, in time, that his packaging business was built
on the site of a defunct agrochemical plant that had once
produced a family of pesticides. The suit claimed that
some deadly runoff had been released into the stream
running through the company property. Had Stewart
looked deeply enough prior to the acquisition, he would
have learned about the pesticides. Regrettably, under EPA
regulations, his company could be liable for the actions of
some long-departed party at this defunct chemical company. Undoubtedly, thorough research would have revealed the business lines of earlier tenants, and perhaps
their waste treatment practices as well. Nothing happens
in a vacuum, finally, and paper trails are easy enough to
follow, even years after they were created.

Increasingly the corporate research techniques employed
in competitive intelligence are employed to clear the path
for acquisitions. Some people call this due diligence re-

search, but to most of us it is only common sense not to buy a pig in a poke.

Due diligence questions can be asked quickly: who are the company's customers, what kind of past and present legal problems exist, what kinds of legal problems might the company expect in the future, what will impinge on a company's profitability down the road, has the company had environmental difficulties? Are key patents about to expire? Are customers about to leave the fold? Have key employees left? How is product quality? Obvious things can easily be overlooked in the heat of an acquisition.

Checklist for due diligence

1. What does the company do? Does it have divisions or branches or subsidiaries?

2. Where is it located?

3. Does the owner hold other companies? How is the ownership structured?

4. What are company sales and income?

5. Has the President or other top management had legal difficulties?

6. What are the company's products? What have its products been in the past?

7. Does the company hold significant patents? When do they expire?

8. Has the company been in legal difficulties? What were they?

9. Does the company produce hazardous waste? How has it been handled?

10. What non-hazardous solid and liquid wastes does the company produce?

11. Is the company located on a river, lake, ocean or other body of water?

12. Has the company been in trouble with state or federal regulatory agencies?

13. Has the company had labor problems?

14. Who are the company's customers? Are they industrial or consumer products?

15. How is the company regarded within its home community?

16. Who are the company's competitors? Where are they located?

17. Is the company well-managed, or is it living on its reputation?

18. What kinds of expertise and technical knowledge are required to run the plant?

19. Are the company's bills being paid on time?

20. Is the target company in the same line of business as the buyer?

21. Have the company's products been portrayed adversely in the media?

22. How old is the plant and the equipment, and how have they been maintained?

23. What kinds of relationships does the company have with its key customers?

24. Have personnel vital to the company's success defected recently? Where did they go?

No tool should be ignored to get the information you need to proceed with some assurance. Using the telephone to get at some of these questions is often the most effective way to proceed. Database searching is vital for local and regional news, credit reports, management profiles, competitor profiles, secretary of state filings, toxic substance regulations, and product defects. Product liability can have an extended half-life—one company found itself paying out $1 million for a defective football helmet 24 years after the product had been produced. The manufacturer of the helmet was buried in an acquisition four layers deep, and nearly a quarter of a century old. "What football helmet?" the latest owner must have thought. Real-life time bombs aren't effective this long, and you can usually hear them ticking.

Corporate patents should also be checked. The company may have a key product whose patent is about to expire. In one case we looked at a company that appeared to hold a valuable patent, but in fact the rights to the patent had been lost in a prior acquisition. The matter had just not been pursued by the acquiring company.

Who are the corporation's primary customers, and how many customers does it have? If the company is losing customers over personnel defections or product defects or whatever, this could have a long term effect on the company's future prospects. Even a multinational corporation can forget to check the customer base.

The recent purchase of Firestone Tire & Rubber Company by the Bridgestone Corporation of Japan is one case of an acquisition complicated by a seemingly inadequate investigation. *The National Review of Corporate Acquisitions*

noted: "The ink was still wet on the $2.6 billion agreement
(to acquire Firestone Tire & Rubber Co.) when General
Motors made the shocking announcement it was dropping
Firestone as one of its key OEM suppliers ... The dumping
of Firestone must have been under high level management
consideration for a long time. Yet Bridgestone got no
inkling of this impending disaster. Whatever happened to
due diligence?" In all fairness, picking up something in a
Detroit auto manufacturer's mind about plans for dropping Firestone, particularly prior to an acquisition by a
Japanese company, might have taken more magic and
prescience than skill in due diligence research.

How dependent is the target company on the skills of one
or two key people? Recent defections of key personnel can
often be tracked via online databases by inputting the
company name and "personnel change" or "personnel" or
"management." If the company deals with high technology or is just running a product that is complex, personnel
changes can spell trouble or even disaster. If the defectors
have gone over to an important competitor, it could be a
disaster. The manager of a multi-layer, high-barrier rigid
plastic container plant whom we interviewed said, "This is
a dangerous product to run. If I look away or blink twice at
the wrong time, I'll wind up with a lot of expensive and
useless plastic. I can't put it back in again. Once it's run,
it's like toothpaste out of the tube."

Human resources are often not properly thought out as a
factor in the deal, to the detriment of all concerned. If
benefits packages are changed or if personnel are kept in
the dark too long about the nature of the deal (who will
stay, who will go, will plants be shut down, is retaining
key management part of the package, etc.), mass defections
can impair the performance and stability of the acquired

company and work its way downstream to the customer in short time. One company we know of did not deal openly with its personnel, and by nearly every criteria we know of, the company's operations hit the skids. Some of the things this involved were: important and not-so-important personnel left; tardiness and sick-leave escalated; theft became rampant; and morale bottomed-out within weeks.

Practically none of this has to happen, but the failure to deal openly with personnel during a time of uncertainty insures that much of it will.

You'll need to talk to people outside the company's walls to determine such things as customer perceptions of a company's industrial or consumer products. These need to be current perceptions. Picking up stray bits of information based on long-standing views of the company and its products is important, but you also need to know if there has been any service or product quality slippage within the past few months. It takes years to build a sound reputation, corporate or individual, and only weeks or months to destroy it.

Environmental due diligence issues
Just a few years ago, deal-makers became concerned with environmental liability primarily in chemical or petroleum deals. Today it is understood that nearly any acquisition can bring substantial environmental risk. A long-buried and long-forgotten gas tank outside the plant garage may be quietly poisoning the water-table for miles around. In addition, every facility that employs baths, coatings, acids, treatments, gels or solvents enjoys the potential for environmental mayhem. The question is further amplified by history—by what has happened in the past—which complicates the detective work by an order of magnitude over

that involved in looking at current practices, but this history question is largely left up to the full process of due diligence later in the deal.

The ghosts of former corporate lives surround every potential acquisition. A cozy bakery may be housed in a building that produced rat poison forty years ago—too long ago for anyone's memory to pick it up. So it is never enough to go by appearances, and assume that since it is only a bakery in a little brick building from the last century, that therefore toxic waste and pollution of the soil and water surrounding the facility are ruled out.

What are the costs of environmental compliance now and in the future? The Resource Conservation and Recovery Act (RCRA, pronounced Ricra) dictates some severe regulations that govern the treatment of hazardous wastes. RCRA could also put some domestic operations at a competitive disadvantage globally. However, if U.S. corporations seem burdened by too much regulation, many European and some Pacific Rim countries are well on their way to similar or worse constraints. We do not yet have "Green" political parties as some European countries do.

A number of federal environmental statutes govern liability for toxic substances pollution.

> **CERCLA**
> Comprehensive Environmental Response, Compensation and Liability Act, or "Superfund Law"—governs soil contamination and resulting groundwater pollution. CERCLA addresses liability for pre-existing hazardous waste disposal sites.

RCRA
Resource Conservation and Recovery Act— .
governs the ongoing generation, transportation,
storage, treatment and disposal of hazardous
wastes.

CWA
Clean Water Act—governs the pollution of
surface water.

SDWA
Safe Drinking Water Act—regulates the quality of
drinking water supplies.

CAA
Clean Air Act—regulates emissions of toxic
pollutants into the atmosphere.

TSCA
Toxic Substances Control Act—regulates PCBs.

Superfund law

CERCLA is intended to facilitate cleanup of hazardous
waste sites. CERCLA provides funds and enforcement
authority that apply to all environmental media: air, water,
and soil. It can apply to industrial, commercial or non-
commercial facilities.

CERCLA provides the government with two methods of
obtaining cleanup of hazardous waste sites. The statute
created a federal fund, called "Superfund" to pay for the
cleanup of sites where hazardous substances have been
released into the environment. Once federal funds have
been spent on cleanup of waste dump sites, the government is entitled to recover those costs from:

- the current owner and operator of the facility
- the owner and operator at the time the waste was disposed of
- the parties that sent wastes to the facility of sited for treatment or disposal
- the person who accepted the wastes for transport to the site if he chose the site.

These parties are liable for all costs of remedial action, any other necessary response costs, and damages for injury to natural resources. The liability of these parties is joint and several, i.e. any one responsible party can be held liable for all of the expense related to a particular site. Moreover, responsible parties are subject to strict liability without regard to fault. Thus the buyer of the property or a persons who contributed only a portion of the hazardous waste found at the site may be held liable for the entire cost of cleanup.

RCRA regulates the ongoing generation, transportation, treatment, storage and disposal of hazardous wastes,with the goal of preventing futures environmental contamination. The RCRA regulatory program consists of:

- record keeping by hazardous waste generators, manifests for waste transporters, and permits for persons treating, storing, or disposing of hazardous waste
- regulation of underground storage tanks for petroleum products and other hazardous materials to prevent environmental damage due to leakage and a ban on dumping of solid (i.e., non-hazardous) waste in un-permitted open dumps.

EPA developed a list of wastes considered hazardous, and additional wastes may be found to be hazardous on the basis of toxicity, corrosivity, reactivity or ignitability characteristics. Facilities generating hazardous wastes are required to: notify the EPA of the waste generation, handle wastes properly, keep records of wastes produced and shipped, store wastes for no more than 90 days, and dispose of wastes at a RCRA permitted disposal facility.

The most common type of environmental liability faced by an acquisition is pre-existing soil contamination. While past acts by previous owners or operators resulting in air or water pollution are unlikely to produce lingering contamination of the site, discharge of pollutants into the soil, and any groundwater aquifers lying beneath the soil, is likely to result in long term contamination.

Not so long ago, finding out if a certain company or location or owner had environmental problems meant contacting the EPA, which often consumed considerable time. Now, fortunately, there is an online database, or a series of databases, available through Mead Data Central's LEXIS-NEXIS, that can answer many waste, pollution, SuperFund and environmental questions. The library is called VISTA, and the information resides in a group of files known as ENVIRN. We will not detail the individual files here, but there are a number of kinds of access to the files that may be of interest. For example: one can search online by the EPA identification number; by an official or individual owner of the facility; or even by the longitude and latitude of the location. LEXIS-NEXIS has a pamphlet describing the VISTA library in detail.

Some final thoughts

Information is where you find it, as we've said before. Perhaps that is just another way of describing competitive intelligence. It means finding the information you need in order to do something positive or to avoid something harmful to the company. It means empowerment. Rules, and strategies, apply, just as in any other activity.

Information creates power—and blunts the power of others. One recent study, cited by Benjamin and Tamar Gilad, looked at four successful companies and four struggling ones. One factor common to the successful four was that they valued competitive information highly. The weakest of the successful four had a stronger competitive intelligence program than the strongest of the struggling four. So a strong competitive intelligence function can be an indicator of corporate health.

But if CI is so important, why isn't it more widely known, more widely used? One answer is positive; the other, negative. Positive: CI has been practiced for a long time under many names, or no name at all, just smart management. Managers have always needed information, and they have always found ways (like an informal network of sharp people) of getting that information. In the last few years, people have begun formalizing competitive intelligence and talking about it as a discipline, even a profession. So CI has become a consensus name for a tried-and-true management technique.

The negative answer is that CI is a "hard sell" to managers who do not always appreciate its value. For a CI practitioner to break through into a manager's trusted network of information providers, the CI input must be palpably useful. "Actionable" is the buzz word: you can take the knowledge and use it, if not right away, then for strategic purposes in the foreseeable future.

Competitive intelligence research requires an openness of thought, because you may be looking for things neither you nor your client—nor even the competition—have thought of yet. New possibilities. Ways the market is beginning to move. Signs of difficulty ahead that the market is sensing but no one has quite put together. And in the shorter range, small indications that can be combined to reveal useful facts. You still need to search with a clear and specific focus. Otherwise, it is too easy to waste money. But you need to be alert to coming at the problem at a slightly different angle—focused but a different focus, from a different perspective perhaps.

J

Japan Aviation News: Wing, 90
Japan Computer Industry Scan, 89
Japan Economic Daily, 89
Japan Economic Journal, 89
Japan Economic Newswire, 89
Japan Free Press, 89
Japan High Tech Review, 89
Japan Semiconductor Scan, 90
Japan Weekly Monitor, 90
Japanese Industry Competitive Intelligence
    Tracking Service, 90
JAPIO, 90, 92
JED/Japan Economic Daily, 90
JETRO ACE, 90
JICST, 91, 92
JIJI Stock Price Data Bank, 90

K

KENS/Kyodo English News Service, 91
KOMPASS UK, 72

M

M&A FILINGS, 72
Main Economic Indicators
    Historical Statistics, 1960-1979, 136
Major Companies of the Arab World, 132
Major Companies of the Far East, 132
Market Search (Maaketto Sachi), 95
Markets of Asia Pacific
    People's Republic of China, 140
MARS, 77

Y
Yearbook of International Trade Statistics, 137
Yearbook of Labor Statistics, 137

About the Authors

RICHARD E. COMBS did his undergraduate work at
Indiana University and took his Master's degree from
Columbia University in the City of New York. He has
headed several major public libraries, among them
Newport, R.I.; Northbrook, Illinois; Gary, Indiana; and
the Chicago Public Library's Cultural Center. He is the
author of an award-winning reference/research book.
His articles have appeared in such widely divergent
publications as *Database* magazine, *Cosmopolitan,* and
Road & Track. He has written major industry studies on
glass and plastic packaging, environmental marketing,
and chemical industry dynamics.

JOHN D. MOORHEAD did his undergraduate work at
Columbia University in the City of New York and took
his Master's degree from Duke University. He was an air
intelligence officer in the U. S. Navy and later a staff
reporter for *The Christian Science Monitor,* writing extensively on business issues for the *Monitor.* Mr. Moorhead's
articles on business research and competitive intelligence
have appeared in *Marketing News* and *Competitor Intelligence.* Mr. Moorhead has prepared studies on the food,
electronics, and clothing industries.

Richard E. Combs and John D. Moorhead are partners in
CombsMoorhead Associates, Inc., a business research
firm in Chicago.